NUTRITION & HEALTH

Childhood Obesity

NUTRITION & HEALTH

Childhood Obesity

LEANNE K. CURRIE-MCGHEE

LUCENT BOOKS
A part of Gale, Cengage Learning

GALE
CENGAGE Learning·

Detroit • New York • San Francisco • New Haven, Conn • Waterville, Maine • London

LIBRARY OF CONGRESS CATALOGING-IN-PUBLICATION DATA

Currie-McGhee, L. K. (Leanne K.)
 Childhood obesity / by Leanne K. Currie-McGhee.
   p. cm. -- (Nutrition and health)
 Summary: "Each title in the series delves into some of the hottest nutrition and health topics being discussed today. The series also provides readers with tools for evaluating conflicting and ever-changing ideas about nutrition and health"-- Provided by publisher.
 Includes bibliographical references and index.
 ISBN 978-1-4205-0723-2 (hardback)
1. Obesity in children--Juvenile literature. I. Title.
 RJ399.C6C87 2012
 618.92'398--dc23
                                                              2012002939

Lucent Books
27500 Drake Rd.
Farmington Hills, MI 48331

ISBN-13: 978-1-4205-0723-2
ISBN-10: 1-4205-0723-0

Printed in the United States of America
1 2 3 4 5 6 7 16 15 14 13 12

TABLE OF CONTENTS

Many people today are often amazed by the amount of nutrition and health information, often contradictory, that can be found in the media. Television, newspapers, and magazines bombard readers with the latest news and recommendations. Television news programs report on recent scientific studies. The healthy living sections of newspapers and magazines offer information and advice. In addition, electronic media such as websites, blogs, and forums post daily nutrition and health news and recommendations.

This constant stream of information can be confusing. The science behind nutrition and health is constantly evolving. Current research often leads to new ideas and insights. Many times, the latest nutrition studies and health recommendations contradict previous studies or traditional health advice. When the media reports these changes without giving context or explanations, consumers become confused. In a survey by the National Health Council, for example, 68 percent of participants agreed that "when reporting medical and health news, the media often contradict themselves, so I don't know what to believe." In addition, the Food Marketing Institute reported that eight out of ten consumers thought it was likely that nutrition and health experts would have a completely different idea about what foods are healthy within five years. With so much contradictory information, people have difficulty deciding how to apply nutrition and health recommendations to their lives. Students find it difficult to find relevant, yet clear and credible information for reports.

Changing recommendations for antioxidant supplements are an example of how confusion can arise. In the 1990s antioxidants such as vitamins C and E and beta-carotene came to the public's attention. Scientists found that people who ate more antioxidant-rich foods had a lower risk of heart disease, cancer, vision loss, and other chronic conditions than those who ate lower amounts. Without waiting for more scientific study, the media and supplement companies quickly spread the word that antioxidants could help fight and prevent disease. They recommended that people take antioxidant supplements and eat fortified foods. When further scientific studies were completed, however, most did not support the initial recommendations. While naturally occurring antioxidants in fruits and vegetables may help prevent a variety of chronic diseases, little scientific evidence proved antioxidant supplements had the same effect. In fact, a study published in the November 2008 *Journal of the American Medical Association* found that supplemental vitamins A and C gave no more heart protection than a placebo. The study's results contradicted the widely publicized recommendation, leading to consumer confusion. This example highlights the importance of context for evaluating nutrition and health news. Understanding a topic's scientific background, interpreting a study's findings, and evaluating news sources are critical skills that help reduce confusion.

Lucent's Nutrition and Health series is designed to help young people sift through the mountain of confusing facts, opinions, and recommendations. Each book contains the most recent up-to-date information, synthesized and written so that students can understand and think critically about nutrition and health issues. Each volume of the series provides a balanced overview of today's hot-button nutrition and health issues while presenting the latest scientific findings and a discussion of issues surrounding the topic. The series provides young people with tools for evaluating conflicting and ever-changing ideas about nutrition and health. Clear narrative peppered with personal anecdotes, fully documented primary and secondary source quotes, informative sidebars, fact boxes, and statistics are all used to help readers understand these topics and how they affect their bodies and their lives. Each volume includes information about changes in trends over time, political controversies, and international perspectives. Full-color photographs and charts enhance all volumes in the series. The Nutrition and Health series is a valuable resource for young people to understand current topics and make informed choices for themselves.

A Modern Childhood

American children lived very different lives in the 1800s than they do today. Back then, a typical child spent much of his or her time doing chores. Children walked to school or to visit friends, and they played active, outdoor games for entertainment. Children's diets consisted of fresh, seasonal fruits, vegetables, and meat instead of processed foods. They did not typically eat foods that contained a lot of sugar. As a result of their eating habits and physical activity levels, most children during these times maintained a healthy weight and were not in danger of becoming overweight or obese.

Modern American children lead quite different lives. Most children spend about eight hours per day sitting in school classrooms. Many schools do not require students to participate in physical education classes or outdoor recess on a daily basis. When they get home from school, or on summer vacation, many children fill their free time with non-active forms of entertainment, such as television, computers, and video games. Children of today also eat different foods than their ancestors did. Many children eat fast food on a regular basis and consume large quantities of sugary beverages. They rarely eat the recommended amounts of fruits and vegetables. This combination of unhealthy eating habits and lack of exercise has affected the physical development and health of millions of American children.

"Throughout most of human history, calories were relatively scarce and hard to get, and physical activity was unavoidable (it was called survival)," explained Dr. David Katz, director of the Yale Prevention Research Center. "We now find ourselves in a modern world in which physical activity is scarce and hard to get, and calories are all but unavoidable. We have no native defenses against such forces, and so an overwhelming majority of us are succumbing to them. No character flaw required. Just timing. All that is required is to be a citizen of the modern world."[1]

A Problem for All

Americans are not the only ones struggling with weight issues. Changes in lifestyle and eating habits have made obesity a major problem for adults and children all over the world. The United States is one of seven countries in which 20 percent or more of the population is obese (the others are Australia, Greece, Mexico, New Zealand, Slovakia, and the United Kingdom). The World Health Organization (WHO) predicts that obesity may soon pass infectious disease as the top cause of health ailments worldwide.

What many health professionals find most alarming is that rates of childhood obesity are increasing every year. An estimated 12.5 million American children and adolescents between the ages of two and nineteen—17 percent of the total population in this age group—are obese. An additional 15 percent of children in this age group are at risk of becoming obese or overweight. "Today, obesity is considered a public-health threat, the toll of a toxic environment that endangers the well-being of our children and their future," wrote Claudia Kalb in *Newsweek*. "Urbanization, modernization, technology, and the globalization of food markets . . . has created a crisis of 'epidemic proportions,' in the words of the World Health Organization."[2]

Obese children face a number of physical, social, and emotional problems that can persist into adulthood. Obesity increases the likelihood that children will encounter health problems that once affected mainly adults, such as diabetes and high blood pressure. Researchers also have found that children who are obese generally have lower self-esteem than their peers, which affects their school performance, social interactions, and overall well-being. In addition, they are more likely to be subjected to teasing or bullying.

Lesley Kinzel remembers what it was like to be an obese child. She stopped playing sports and being active because she worried about other people's reactions to her weight. "Prior to being told I was fat by my well-intentioned pediatrician (who showed me how far outside the standard 'height-weight' guidelines I fell for my age), I'd spent my life as an

The United States is one of seven countries in which 20 percent of the population is obese.

active and athletic child," she recalled. "As I got older I came to understand what being fat meant: fat kids were lousy at sports, and those who tried to play were to be mocked for it. . . . So I stopped playing. I backed away from sports and games altogether."[3]

Like many other obese children, Kinzel has continued to deal with weight issues in adulthood. To prevent this from happening, experts say children and families must adopt healthy eating habits and lead an active lifestyle. The sooner these changes are made in a child's life, the better the child's chances of reaching a healthy weight—and maintaining a healthy weight into adulthood. It is possible to stop the epidemic of childhood obesity. It is also essential if future generations are to enjoy long and healthy lives.

CHAPTER 1

A Growing Problem

D r. Elsie Taveras, codirector of the Obesity Prevention Program at the Harvard Medical School, has seen the worst effects of obesity among children. One day she watched a four-year-old boy walk into her clinic with a limp. "He was carrying so much weight, he displaced his hips,"[4] said Taveras. The boy weighed more than 100 pounds (45kg) and had a body mass index (BMI) that was over the 99th percentile for his age group.

This boy's struggles with obesity were extreme, but not as unusual as they once would have been. Childhood obesity has emerged as a serious problem all over the world. In 2010, the World Health Organization reported that more than 40 million children worldwide were overweight. Obesity is especially problematic in industrialized countries like the United States. Over 12.5 million American children are considered obese by medical standards, and obesity rates among teens and children have nearly tripled in the United States since 1980.

The two primary reasons for the rising numbers of overweight and obese children are lack of physical exercise and poor eating habits. Studies indicate that only about 18 percent of adolescents living in the United States get one hour of physical activity per day, and only about 22 percent eat

five or more servings of fruits and vegetables per day. Unless Americans make major changes to their children's nutrition and exercise patterns, the problem of childhood obesity will likely continue to grow.

Changes in Diet Worsen Obesity Crisis

One of the main reasons that childhood obesity has become such a major problem in the world is an overall change in people's diets, particularly in industrialized countries like the United States. People in industrialized countries have greater access to processed foods, such as packaged snacks and meals. In addition, more people eat food outside of their homes. Typically, the food purchased at fast-food restaurants and other food-service outlets is higher in calories and lower in nutritional value than home-cooked food. A 2011 University of North Carolina study found that the percentage of calories children consumed away from home—such as at restaurants and at school—increased from 23.4 percent to

A lack of physical exercise and poor eating habits are the primary reasons for the rising numbers of obese children in the United States.

33.9 percent from 1977 to 2006. Partly as a result, children's food consumption increased by an average of 179 calories per day during this same period.

Specifically, fast food has become a major source of people's food intake, and this type of food is typically high in fat and low in nutrition. According to the Children's Defense Fund, fast-food consumption has increased fivefold among children in the United States since 1970. Nearly one-third of American children ages four to nineteen eat fast food every day, resulting in a weight gain of about 6 extra pounds (2.72kg) per year for each child. A related concern is that children are eating fewer fruits and vegetables than in the past.

Besides eating foods with lower nutritional value, children and adults today typically eat larger portions of food than earlier generations. A 2002 study by New York University's Department of Nutrition and Food Studies found a general increase in portion sizes at all types of eating establishments. Restaurants use larger dinner plates, bakeries use larger muffin tins, pizzerias use larger pans, and fast-food companies use larger containers for drinks and french fries.

The study also found that unlike fifteen to twenty-five years ago, food companies now use larger sizes as selling points to attract customers. In the mid-1950s, for example, McDonald's offered only one size of french fries. That size is now considered Small, and it is one-third the weight of the largest size available, known as Supersize. The Supersize portion of fries contains 610 calories, compared to 210 calories for a Small. Since people are naturally inclined to eat the amount of food placed in front of them, increased portion sizes typically lead to increased caloric intake.

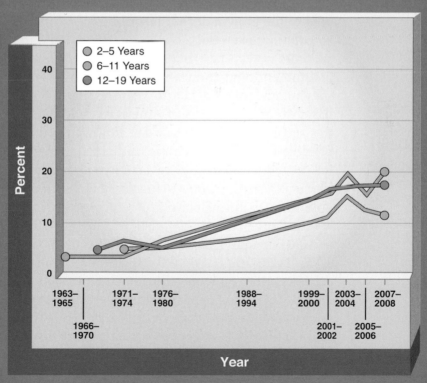

Trends in Obesity Among Children and Adolescents

Note: Obesity is defined as body mass index (BMI) greater than or equal to sex- and age-specific 95th percentile from the 2000 Centers for Disease Control and Prevention (CDC) Growth Charts.

Taken from: CDC/NCHS, National Health Examination Surveys II (ages 6–11), III (ages 12–17), and National Health and Nutrition Examination Surveys (NHANES) I–III, and NHANES 1999–2000, 2001–2002, 2003–2004, 2005–2006, and 2007–2008. www.cdc.gov/nchs/data/hestat/obesity_child_07_08/obesity_child_07_08.htm, p. 3.

Modern families also eat fewer meals together. Some experts believe that this trend also contributes to the obesity problem. "The frequency of shared family meals is significantly related to nutritional health in children and adolescents," wrote Amber J. Hammons and Barbara H. Fiese in *Pediatrics* magazine. "Children and adolescents who share family meals three or more times per week are more likely to be in a normal weight range and have healthier dietary and eating patterns than those who share fewer than three family meals together."[5] A 2010 study called *The Importance of Family Dinners VI,* conducted by the National Center on Addiction and Substance Abuse at Columbia University, found that 60 percent of teens eat dinner with their families at least five times per week, while 40 percent of teens have family dinners between zero and four times per week.

Lack of Exercise

Lack of exercise is another important factor that has contributed to the growth of childhood obesity. Gym class, recess, and outdoor play after school were common pastimes among students in years past, but this is no longer the case. Experts recommend that children ages six to nineteen should get sixty minutes of moderate-to-vigorous physical activity most days. About two-thirds of American children do not meet this recommendation every day, however, and one-quarter of adolescents do not achieve this level on any day. Reasons for the reduction in physical activity range from fewer gym classes offered at schools to increased use of electronics over outdoor play during periods of leisure activity.

Only slightly more than half of students nationwide are enrolled in a physical education (PE) class. By high school, according to the National Association for Sport and Physical Education, only one-third of students take a gym class daily. While many public health experts and physicians recommend daily gym class from kindergarten through high school, Illinois is the only state to require daily PE for all class levels. Most schools have either cut gym class entirely or reduced it to once or twice a week. This reduction is mainly due to budget cuts and pressure on schools to meet government academic performance standards.

Breast or Bottle?

Doctors have long recommended that women breast-feed their babies because of the nutrition and immunities that breast milk provides. In addition, studies now show that breast-fed babies have a lower risk of becoming obese than formula-fed babies. According to Joan Younger Meek of the United States Breastfeeding Committee, "Multiple studies have shown that a history of not breastfeeding increases the risk of being overweight or obese in childhood and adolescence. Adolescent obesity often persists into adult life. Breastfeeding plays an important role in obesity prevention and improving overall health outcomes, and therefore is vitally important to public health." Studies also show that the longer and the more exclusively babies breastfeed, the better their health outcomes in terms of weight. Despite the many benefits, however, most babies in the United States do not get their nutrients primarily from breastfeeding. According to the U.S. Centers for Disease Control and Prevention (CDC), 75 percent of American babies start out being breast-fed, but only 15 percent are exclusively breast-fed at six months of age.

United States Breastfeeding Committee. "Preventing Obesity at Birth Through Breastfeeding." February 11, 2010. www.usbreastfeeding.org/NewsInformation /NewsRoom/201002PreventingObesityBeginsatBirth/tabid/169/Default.aspx.

Some schools also do not regularly schedule recess, citing the need to spend more time on academics. Yet many experts say that cutting recess not only contributes to obesity but also inhibits academic performance. "Physical activity is essential for healthy growth and development," wrote Ben and Lisa Dyson in the *Commercial Appeal*. "Research has overwhelmingly found recess benefits the health of elementary school–age children through increased aerobic endurance, muscular strength and coordination, and control of excess weight gain and its related health problems."[6] Recess also has been linked to better academic performance. Studies show that children are able to concentrate better after exercising their bodies.

Many American children do not get enough exercise after school, either. Rather than playing outside or participating in team sports, an increasing number of children spend a great percentage of their free time watching television or playing video games. One study found that kids younger than six spend an average of 2 hours per day in front of a screen, mostly watching television or movies. Older kids and teens spend almost 4 hours per day watching TV or movies. When computer use and video games are included, the time spent in front of a screen increases to over 5.5 hours per day. The American Academy of Pediatrics (AAP) suggests that parents limit children to a total of 1 to 2 hours of screen time per day. Excessive screen time reduces children's opportunities for active, creative play and thus contributes to obesity.

Stress and Depression

Today more children struggle with stress, anxiety, and depression than in decades past. One study found that 8 percent of the U.S. population ages twelve to seventeen experienced a depressive episode in 2009, meaning that they experienced five or more symptoms of depression most of the time for at least two weeks. According to a 2009 Iowa State University survey, increased levels of stress in adolescents are associated with a greater likelihood of obesity. For example, 47 percent of the teens in the overall sample were overweight or obese, but this percentage increased to 56.2 percent among survey respondents who were affected by four or more "stressors." As lead author Brenda Lohman stated, "an adolescent or youth who's more stressed—caused by such things as having poor grades, mental health problems, more aggressive behavior, or doing more drugs and alcohol—is also more likely to be overweight or obese."[7]

Other studies have uncovered links between depression and obesity. In 2010 Floriana S. Luppino and a team

FOOD FACT

In the early 1990s, the average bagel sold in the United States was 3 inches (7.6cm) in diameter and provided 140 calories. Today, the average bagel is 6 inches (15.2cm) in diameter and contains 350 calories.

People who experience depression or stress may gain weight because they are more likely to overeat and to avoid exercising.

of researchers at Leiden University Medical Center in the Netherlands analyzed the results of fifteen previous studies involving 58,745 participants. "We found bidirectional [two-way] associations between depression and obesity: obese persons had a 55 percent increased risk of developing depression over time, whereas depressed persons had a 58 percent increased risk of becoming obese,"[8] said the authors of the study.

People who experience depression or stress may gain weight because they are more likely to overeat, make poor food choices, avoid exercise, and become sedentary (inactive). In addition, researchers have found that people with depression have decreased levels of serotonin, an important hormone. Serotonin is a chemical produced in the brain that influences both mood and appetite. Low serotonin levels have been associated with a higher risk for obesity. Some people with depression may overeat in a subconscious attempt to restore their serotonin levels to normal and improve their mood.

Who Is at Risk?

Some children are more at risk of becoming obese than others. Children whose parents are obese, for example, are more likely to become obese than those whose parents fall within a normal weight range. According to the American Academy of Child and Adolescent Psychiatry, if one parent is obese, there is a 50 percent chance that his or her children will also be obese. When both parents are obese, their children have an 80 percent chance of being obese.

This tendency for obesity to run in families is due both to genetic and environmental factors. In terms of environment, children typically eat in a similar way as their parents. So if the parents eat larger portions or less healthy food, it is likely that the children will too. Parents also serve as role models for their children in terms of activity levels and exercise habits. Children who grow up in households where the parents do not exercise are less likely to establish healthy exercise patterns.

Studies also indicate that there is a genetic link to obesity. The genes children inherit from their parents influence their body type, fat mass, growth rate, appetite, and metabolism. As a result, children of obese parents are genetically more inclined to become obese. The fact that these children have an increased risk of obesity does not mean they are destined to become obese, however. With proper exercise and nutrition, doctors state that many children with genetic risk factors can still maintain a healthy weight.

Racial and Economic Factors

Obesity affects boys and girls of all ages, races, ethnic groups, and income levels throughout the United States and the world. However, some groups are more affected than others. Race appears to be a factor in determining a child's likelihood of being overweight or obese. According to the Children's Defense Fund, African American and Hispanic American children are more at risk for being overweight and obese than white children. Specifically, research shows that 1 out of every 5 black children ages two to nineteen is obese, compared to approximately 1 out of every 7 white children.

Because parents serve as role models for their kids, parents who eat healthfully and exercise are less likely to have children with weight problems.

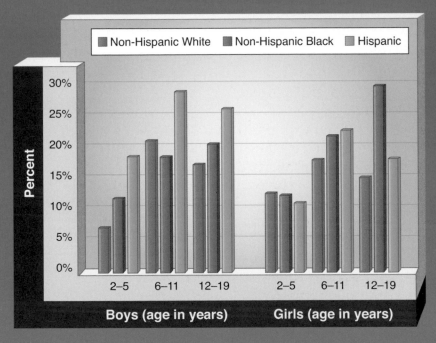

Prevalence of Obesity, Children and Teens, 2007–2008

This bar chart breaks down childhood obesity in the United States by race and gender.

■ Non-Hispanic White   ■ Non-Hispanic Black   ■ Hispanic

Percent

30%
25%
20%
15%
10%
5%
0%

2–5   6–11   12–19   2–5   6–11   12–19

Boys (age in years)   **Girls (age in years)**

Taken from: Cynthia L. Ogden. "Childhood Obesity in the United States: The Magnitude of the Problem." www.cdc.gov/about/grand-rounds/archives/2010/download/GR-062010.pdf, page 14.

Economics is another factor that influences whether children will experience weight problems. Studies have found that almost 45 percent of overweight or obese children ages ten to seventeen are poor. There are many possible reasons for this breakdown. Some studies have found that poorer children are obese not because they overeat, but because they eat food that is not nutritious. According to Dr. Roberto Trevino, director of the nonprofit Social and Health Research Center, a nine-year-old should consume 1,400 to 2,200 calories daily to sustain growth. A 2008 study of 1,400 inner-city children in San Antonio, Texas, found that 44 percent consumed fewer than 1,400 calories a day. Even with this low caloric intake, however, 33 percent of those studied were obese. "They were not overeating," Trevino said. "These kids were not eating enough, and when they did eat it was all the wrong things."[9]

The study found that there were four key nutrients missing from the children's diets: calcium, magnesium, potassium, and phosphorus. Each nutrient plays an important role in how the body functions. Magnesium, for instance, is involved in more than three hundred enzymatic reactions in the body that help to regulate metabolism and cell function. When magnesium—which is found in spinach, broccoli, black beans, bran cereal, nuts, fish, and other foods—is missing from the diet, it can predispose an individual to obesity and related health disorders, such as diabetes.

Several other factors may contribute to the higher rates of obesity among poor children. Studies have found that children in predominantly minority and low-income neighborhoods have reduced access to supermarkets and other sources of fresh produce. Low-income families also tend to eat more fast food because it is inexpensive and convenient. However, fast food is typically high in fat and low in nutrition compared to home-cooked meals. Inner-city children also have less access to safe outdoor play areas, which limits their opportunities to exercise. Nearly 90 percent of the children in the San Antonio study, for instance, received marginal or unacceptable scores on physical fitness tests. Without early intervention, Trevino predicted that some of the children will develop cardiovascular health problems that would require open-heart surgery by the time they reached the age of twenty-five.

Babies at Risk

Some babies may face an increased risk of obesity even before they are born. Studies show that a mother's eating habits dur-

> # FOOD FACT
>
> Adolescents between the ages of eight and eighteen spend an average of 7.5 hours per day using entertainment media, including TV, computers, video games, cell phones, and movies.

ing pregnancy affect her unborn child. According to research published in the journal *Diabetes* in 2011, expectant mothers who ate diets lower in vegetables, fruits, whole grains, and other carbohydrates during pregnancy produced subtle changes in their babies' DNA in the womb. These changes influenced the development of the babies' metabolism and increased the tendency of their bodies to store fat. As a result, the children studied were likely to be heavier and have a higher percentage of body fat at age nine. They also faced a higher risk of obesity, heart disease, and diabetes later in life.

Once born, a baby's risk of attaining an unhealthy weight can also increase if the baby is fed too much. Some parents and other adults unintentionally make poor food choices for their babies and toddlers because they equate size with health, and they think the child will eventually lose the baby fat. "There is a popular belief, culturally embedded in our minds, that a chubby baby is a healthy baby, and children will grow out of it," Taveras said. "Those two perceptions are inaccurate."[10] If allowed to continue gaining weight at an unhealthy rate, babies and toddlers are much more likely to grow into overweight or obese adolescents.

In 2011 the U.S. Institute of Medicine released a report on preventing obesity in children under the age of five. The report stated that almost 10 percent of infants and toddlers in the United States carry excess weight for their body length. The authors of the report also found that one in five kids between the ages of two and five is overweight or obese before entering kindergarten.

Medical Issues

In some cases, medical conditions can place children at a higher risk of obesity. Just as depression can contribute to weight gain, so too can low levels of thyroid hormones, sleep problems, certain medications, and other medical issues. Tasha Secuskie grew worried when she noticed that her infant daughter, Tylynn, had gained an unusual 6 pounds (2.7kg) between her sixth and eighth weeks of life. Tylynn's doctors were puzzled as to what had caused such a big weight gain. Then, at eighteen months, Tylynn started gaining weight dramatically once again.

Harmless Toys?

For years, fast-food restaurants such as McDonald's have included toys in their children's meals. TV commercials often highlight these toys in an effort to attract families with young children to fast-food restaurants. Some parents and public interest groups claim that this practice contributes to childhood obesity, and they are calling for restaurants to stop putting toys in children's meals. According to Margo Wootan, nutrition policy director for the Center for Science in the Public Interest,

> Using toys to market unhealthy restaurant meals to kids exploits children, annoys parents, and is frowned upon by nutritionists, behavioral

scientists, and a growing number of public health officials around the country. It's too bad that McDonald's, Burger King, Wendy's, and Taco Bell think they can't compete on the basis of quality, value, taste, or nutrition, but instead must resort to such a discredited marketing tactic to lure families to their businesses.

In 2011 the popular hamburger chain Jack in the Box stopped including toys in its kids' meals. Many consumers would like to see America's other major fast-food chains follow suit.

Margo G. Wootan. "Fast Food Chain Drops Toys from Kids' Meals." Center for Science in the Public Interest, June 21, 2011. www.cspinet.org/new/201106211.html.

To market their children's meals, fast-food chains include toys with the meals, a practice deplored by nutritionists, public health officials, and some parents.

Secuskie followed the doctors' recommendations. She reduced her daughter's food portion sizes and eliminated junk food, but these changes did not stop the rapid weight gain. Her entire family stopped eating fried food and changed their diet to one consisting primarily of fruits, vegetables, and lean meats. They also made sure that Tylynn and her younger sister got enough exercise through dance classes, swim lessons, and hikes. Yet while her sister remained at a healthy weight, Tylynn's weight reached 81 pounds (37kg) by the time she turned four.

At that point, Secuskie learned that her daughter had a rare medical condition called hypometabolism, which made Tylynn's body burn calories very slowly. "It breaks my heart, because people stare at you, like 'What are you feeding that kid?'"[11] her mom said. To deal with this issue, Tylynn's parents must be extra vigilant about how much she eats and exercises.

Rising Obesity Rates Around the World

For many years childhood obesity seemed to be mainly an American problem. In the twenty-first century, however, it increasingly has become a worldwide issue. One reason is that many people around the world have copied the dietary patterns of the United States. "Changes are due to rising affluence [wealth], as people in formerly impoverished places gain the means to eat more meat and processed foods—and then fast food starts popping up on the menu,"[12] according to an article in the *New York Times* teen newsmagazine *Upfront*.

As developing nations become better off economically, their populations change what they eat—often with negative consequences. "They replace grains and beans with foods obtained from animal sources," added *Upfront*. "They buy more sweets and more processed foods. Soon they eat more food in general. They often become overweight and develop heart disease, diabetes, and other chronic illnesses common in industrialized societies."[13]

Research shows that people in countries like China and Japan, where the dietary staples were rice and vegetables for many generations, have become heavier as a result of eat-

ing more meat and fast food. In many nations, economic development has also resulted in less physical activity and more sedentary lifestyles. As countries grow more prosperous, more people work at desk jobs in office buildings and fewer people support themselves through manual labor in farm fields and factories. Wealthier populations are also able to buy cars, refrigerators, computers, and other technological devices that make travel, food preparation, and communication easier and less physically demanding.

In China evidence of these dietary and cultural changes can be seen in the nation's children. According to 2007 figures from the Chinese Health Ministry, urban Chinese boys were 2.5 inches (6.35cm) taller and 6.6 pounds (3kg) heavier on average at age six than Chinese city boys were thirty years ago. Today, 8 percent of ten- to twelve-year-olds in China's cities are considered obese and an additional 15 percent are overweight.

Research shows that people in China and Japan have become heavier as a result of trending toward a Western diet, which includes more meat and fast food.

Greece is another country struggling with childhood obesity. Antonis Zampelas of the Agricultural University of Athens has undertaken studies about the rising rates of childhood obesity in his country. He notes that the traditional Mediterranean diet consumed by generations of Greeks—vegetables, legumes (beans, lentils, peas), dairy products, fish, bread, and nuts—has long been associated with low rates of heart disease and other health problems associated with obesity. As people in Greece have moved away from the Mediterranean diet to eat more fatty and salty foods, however, obesity rates have soared. A 2011 Greek Childhood Obesity (GRECO) study indicated that only 4 percent of Greek children adhered to the traditional Mediterranean diet. The study also found that about one-third of Greek children were overweight and about 12 percent were obese. The current childhood obesity rates in Greece are among the highest in Europe.

As the childhood obesity crisis spreads around the world, millions of children are at risk for lifelong health problems. Their emotional welfare is also at stake, since obesity in childhood has been linked to a variety of mental health and behavioral issues. Nations that fail to address this public health crisis risk losing entire generations of youth to lives of diminished health and productivity.

CHAPTER 2

Are You Obese?

By age thirteen, Tara had reached 338 pounds (153kg). She had known she was obese for years, and she had often endured teasing or thoughtless comments about her weight. "I'm so overweight and I get teased constantly and it never stops," she commented in the book *Overweight: What Kids Say.* "When I was in first grade the teasing started. . . . I got teased because I was a lot bigger than everyone else . . . so I just ate more and more and got fatter and fatter."[14]

To prevent their children from dealing with what Tara faced as a teenager experts say parents should consult a doctor as soon as they begin to notice excessive weight gain. A doctor can use measuring tools and growth charts to diagnose whether a child is a healthy weight, overweight, or obese. The earlier a child is diagnosed with obesity, the medical community agrees, the better his or her health outcomes are likely to be. It is easier for children to change unhealthy habits at a younger age, before the habits become ingrained.

What Is Obesity?

Whether or not a person is medically considered obese is determined by their body fat percentage and other health measurements. The most common tool that doctors and

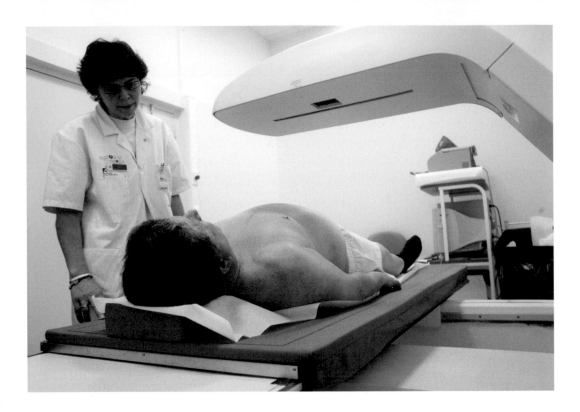

Through the use of dual-energy X-ray absorptiometry, a health care worker determines an obese man's body mass index and his bone density.

other health professionals use to determine if a child is overweight is a body mass index (BMI) chart. BMI is a number that is calculated from a child's weight and height. A number of Internet sites offer free, easy-to-use BMI calculators for both children and adults. The Centers for Disease Control and Prevention (CDC), the American Academy of Pediatrics (AAP), and other organizations of health professionals consider BMI to be a reliable indicator of the percentage of body fat for most children and teens. Although BMI does not measure body fat directly, research has shown that BMI usually correlates with direct methods of measuring body fat, such as underwater weighing.

After a child's BMI has been calculated, the number is plotted on a growth chart that shows the range of BMI values for children of the same age and sex. The result is called a BMI-for-age percentile. A child or adolescent is considered obese if his or her BMI number falls above the 95th percentile of the BMI range for his or her age. Children and teens are considered overweight if their BMI falls between the 85th and 95th percentiles on the BMI-for-age chart. A BMI between the 5th and 85th percentiles places a young person in the healthy weight range, while a BMI below the 5th percentile is considered underweight.

As an example, consider a ten-year-old boy. If he has a BMI of 23 or more, he falls within the upper 5 percent on the BMI-for-age chart and is considered obese. Many different

Body Mass Index-for-Age Percentiles

This chart plots various possible BMI-for-age percentiles for a 10-year-old boy.

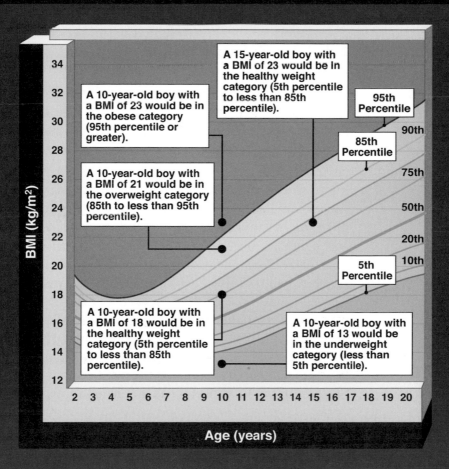

combinations of height and weight can result in a BMI of 23 for a ten-year-old boy. The boy could be 4 feet, 10 inches (147cm) tall and weigh 110 pounds (50kg), or he could be 4 feet, 6 inches (137cm) tall and weigh 95 pounds (43kg). For children and teens, however, age is an important factor in BMI measurements. A fifteen-year-old boy with a BMI of 23, for example, would fall below the 85th percentile on the BMI-for-age chart and be considered a healthy weight.

Although BMI is generally considered an accurate indicator of obesity, certain factors can affect a BMI's reliability. For example, a muscular child might be quite heavy for his or her age and thus have a high BMI. When a child's BMI-for-age percentile is high, health care providers can use further assessments to determine whether or not the child is obese. These assessments may include measuring skinfold thickness, evaluating the child's diet, physical activity level, and family history, or other appropriate health screenings.

More Obese and Overweight Kids

As more pediatricians use BMI to measure children's body fat, more children are being diagnosed with obesity. According to the CDC, the prevalence of obesity among American children aged 6 to 11 years increased from 6.5 percent in 1980 to 19.6 percent in 2008. The prevalence of obesity among adolescents aged 12 to 19 years increased from 5.0 percent to 18.1 percent over that same time period.

More children are being diagnosed as overweight as well. The CDC has reported that 34 percent of all American children are overweight or obese. The greatest risk for an overweight child is that he or she will become obese and develop the health problems associated with obesity. According to the U.S. Department of Health and Human Services, overweight adolescents have a 70 percent chance of becoming overweight or obese adults. The likelihood increases to 80 percent if one or more of the teen's parents is overweight or obese.

The AAP considers the growing number of children who are diagnosed as overweight and obese to be a serious medical problem. The organization actively encourages its sixty thousand member pediatricians to assess children's growth regularly and act promptly to address weight issues with their parents or guardians. It recommends that health care providers plot BMI for their patients beginning at age two and discuss the percentile figures with their parents at each office visit.

The AAP recommends that pediatricians take a variety of actions to address potential weight problems if a patient's BMI-for-age falls between the 85th and 94th percentiles, which places the patient in the overweight category. These actions include encouraging parents to make sure the child is getting the recommended five servings of fruits and vegetables and one hour of physical activity per day. If these actions

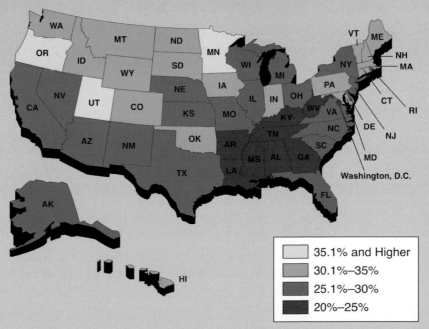

Childhood Overweight and Obesity Trends

This map shows the childhood obesity rate in each state for the year 2007.

35.1% and Higher
30.1%–35%
25.1%–30%
20%–25%

Taken from: National Conference of State Legislatures. Childhood Overweight and Obesity Trends. www.ncsl.org/?tabid=13877.

are not effective and the child's BMI increases to the obese category—in the 95th percentile or above—the AAP recommends that pediatricians provide written diet and exercise plans and schedule more frequent follow-up visits. For patients in the 99th BMI-for-age percentile, pediatricians are urged to consider more aggressive therapies, including medications, diet meal replacements, and even weight-loss surgery in selected adolescents.

Pediatricians must be proactive about dealing with obesity in their patients or else the problems will likely go untreated and get worse. According to a 2010 study by the University of South Florida and Johns Hopkins University, many parents do not fully realize that their children are overweight or obese unless a pediatrician informs them. Yet many pediatricians shy away from discussing children's weight with parents. The North Carolina Child Health Assessment and Monitoring Program (CHAMP) collected height and weight information for 5,699 children from five to seventeen years old between 2007 and 2009. The CHAMP survey also asked parents whether a health care provider had told them that their child was overweight during the past year. Among parents of children whose height and weight placed them in the overweight category, only 11 percent reported that a health care provider had mentioned it. Similarly, only 31 percent of parents of children in the obese category had been informed of this fact by a health care provider.

One reason that doctors may fail to inform parents about their children's weight problems is that they are concerned about the potential for negative reactions. Another reason is that some doctors are unsure whether they can convince the parents to take action. "As a pediatrician, you may ask yourself, 'Do I really want to get into talking about a child's weight with the parent who hasn't asked about it, and if I do, what do I have to offer?'"[15] explained Dr. Raquel Hernandez, assistant professor of pediatrics at the University of South Florida. If doctors do not inform the parents, however, the children are at greater risk for further weight gain and related health problems.

School Testing for Obesity

Many schools across the United States have begun providing information to parents about their children's weight in an effort to increase early intervention rates. As of 2009 twenty states had passed laws requiring BMI assessments or other forms of weight screening in schools. Some schools measure students' body fat during physical fitness tests and send the results home in progress reports for parents to review. Supporters of these programs argue that BMI is a valuable health assessment, and that recognizing the problem is the first step in helping families make necessary lifestyle changes.

Other observers feel that it is inappropriate for schools to evaluate students' weight, however, and the practice remains controversial. Dr. David Herzog, a professor of psychiatry and pediatrics at the Harvard Medical School, believes that schools are the wrong place for body-fat testing. He argues that such tests should only be performed in the privacy of a doctor's office because students who are found to be overweight or obese could become the targets of teasing and bullying by other students. "Doing this in schools seems like a disaster," he said. "Kids knowing these numbers, teasing others who show up with a high BMI or blood pressure, putting the issue of overweight in public view of others when overweight kids have a terrible time in school with teasing."[16]

Another hot debate topic is the practice of using body-fat percentages as a factor in determining students' grades in physical education classes. Hawthorne Elementary School in Elmhurst, Illinois, included a child's BMI as one of six

A doctor checks a girl's body mass index (BMI) with a skinfold gauge.

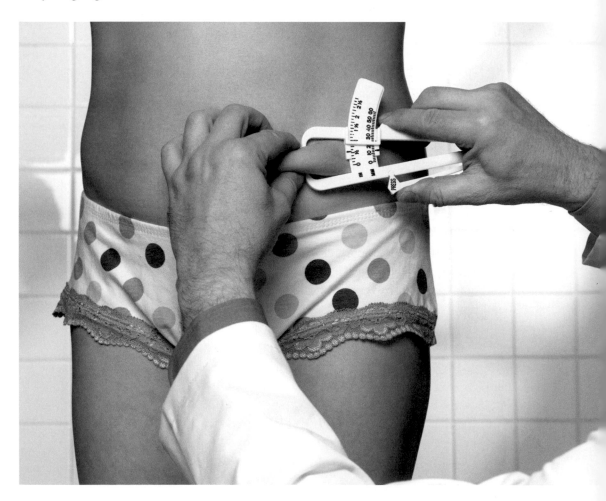

tests used to determine the physical fitness grade on his or her progress report. That practice ended in 2011 when about two dozen parents met with school officials to express their displeasure about how the BMI data was being used. They argued that health issues should be handled by a family doctor, and that the school should not evaluate students on the basis of physical attributes.

Parental Reactions to Childhood Obesity

Many parents find it difficult to hear that their child has been diagnosed as obese. In numerous instances, parents are simply not aware that their child's physical condition is that poor. A 2007 study designed by researchers at the University of Michigan found that many parents did not accurately gauge their child's weight. Among parents of children ages 6 to 11 whose BMI placed them in the category of obese or extremely overweight, 43 percent said their child was "about the right weight," 37 percent responded "slightly overweight," and only 13 percent said "very overweight." Parents of adolescents between the ages of 12 and 17 were slightly more aware of their children's weight problems. Among those with children in the obese or extremely overweight categories, 56 percent said their child was "slightly overweight," 31 percent responded "very overweight," 11 percent said "about the right weight," and 2 percent said "slightly underweight."

The AAP has found that in about half of the cases where a child is obese, one or both of the parents are overweight as well. These parents may find it more difficult to acknowledge or address their children's obesity because it forces them to face up to their own weight problems. In addition, many parents of younger children believe that their extra weight is "baby fat" that will go away as they get older. This view leads some parents to ignore the problem—even after receiving a medical diagnosis of obesity—in hopes that their child will grow out of it. If poor eating habits and a lack of exercise have contributed to the child's obesity, however, the problem will likely get worse if the parents do not make significant changes to their family's lifestyle.

Obesity as a Parental Custody Issue

An article in the July 2011 edition of the *Journal of the American Medical Association* ignited controversy over the degree to which parents should be held responsible for their children's obesity. The authors, Dr. Lindsey Murtagh and Dr. David S. Ludwig of the Harvard School of Public Health, placed a great deal of blame on parents who allowed their children to reach an extreme level of obesity. They suggested that in cases where childhood obesity is linked to major medical problems, authorities should consider removing children from the home and placing them in foster care. Murtagh and Ludwig argued that intervention by Child Protective Services may be the "only realistic way to control harmful behaviors" by parents that lead to morbid obesity in children.

Many parents of overweight and obese children and other health professionals found the article very disturbing. "To equate obesity with parental abuse and neglect seems extreme to me," stated Dr. Gilbert Ross of the American Council on Science and Health. "Child Protective Services is already authorized to remove children from the home if they perceive parental abuse sufficient to rise to a health-threatening situation. To add the morbid obesity issue doesn't really add anything new to these authorities' mission—ensuring that children are provided with a safe and healthy home."

American Council on Science and Health. "A Modest Proposal: JAMA Calls for Removing Obese Children from Their Homes," July 14, 2011. www.acsh.org/facts fears/newsid.2823/news_detail.asp.

The Problem with Nagging

Parental reactions to a child's diagnosis of obesity can have a major impact on the child's self-esteem as well as on his or her chances of attaining a healthy weight. Experts believe that parents should be extremely careful not to nag their child to lose weight. Nagging is often counterproductive. In many instances, nagging actually results in increased caloric intake by children who turn to food for comfort. Nagging and criticism can also harm the parent-child relationship, making a child less likely to confide in parents or go to them for advice on other issues that crop up during their teen years.

At age fifteen, Samantha Kaufman videotaped herself as part of a research project conducted by pediatrician Michael Rich of Children's Hospital Boston to document the difficulties of being an obese teenager. Kaufman complained about what she called relentless nagging by her family about her weight. "If your parents are nagging at you, telling you not to eat something, of course you're going to eat more," she said. Kaufman said the nagging contributed to her developing bulimia, an eating disorder in which episodes

Parental reaction to a child's obesity can have a lasting impact on the child's self-esteem and his or her ability to obtain a healthy weight.

of binge eating are followed by efforts to purge, or get rid of the extra calories consumed. Kaufman forced herself to throw up several times a week because she saw that as the only way she could take control over her body. "I know it's something I can do that nobody else can do,"[17] she explained.

Stephanie Klein, author of the book *Moose: A Memoir of Fat Camp*, was overweight as a child. Her parents often criticized her weight through words or gestures, but their behavior actually drove her to eat more food. "My father would puff out his cheeks at the dinner table. Sometimes I'd just eat to spite him," recalled Klein. "I probably also ate in secrecy because I wasn't free to eat in front of them, in front of my father because he'd be critical. I'd find other ways to get food. I'd have it at school, in the cafeteria, when my parents weren't around."[18]

The Benefits of Encouragement

Health professionals suggest that parents encourage their children to adopt a healthy lifestyle instead of nagging them to lose weight. "We really emphasize to the parents that the most important thing is to keep the focus on their child's health, not their weight," said clinical psychologist Eleanor Mackey. "The last thing we want is for parents to push weight dissatisfaction on kids and have kids feel bad about the way they look."[19]

Pediatricians and other health professionals also urge parents to involve the entire family in developing healthy habits. "For starters, be a very good role model and don't just talk the talk," said Klein. "Don't keep [junk food] in the house. Be active with your child. Show them that you're in it together. It's the whole family that's getting involved, even the thin people in the family. You have to remember it's a health issue; it's not an aesthetic [appearance] issue."[20]

In addition to being active and adopting healthy eating habits as a family, patience is needed to help children get into shape. "It will take longer [to lose weight] if you or your child has been overweight for a longer period of time," according to the Stop Childhood Obesity website. "A good rule of thumb to get back into acceptable shape is one to two months of healthy living for every year of unhealthy living. So, if your child has been overweight for just a year, it will take only two months to get them back down to the proper weight and size."[21] The website suggests that families establish short-term and long-term goals for their members to reach as a team.

Encouraging healthy choices will help children gain confidence and feel good about themselves. The better they feel about themselves, the easier it is to make lasting lifestyle changes rather than resorting to food for emotional comfort. "First of all, tell your child that you love him or her. A support system is the one thing that will get them through this painful process," said a writer for the Healthy Journey website. "They will be dealing with lots of feelings about being overweight. It's not as easy as 'Oh, gee, I'm overweight.' A child's feelings about being obese go much deeper, sometimes affecting how they feel about themselves as a person. They need you to reaffirm that they have worth, at any weight."[22]

Children's Responses to Obesity

Overweight and obese children are usually aware of their problems with weight from an early age, even if they are not explicitly told of their condition by family members or doctors. Obese children generally realize they are heavy based on the standards of physical beauty they see in movies, television shows, and magazines as well as on their own personal interactions with other people who tease them. These interactions can affect how they feel about themselves for years.

For some children, the realization that they are obese or overweight can lead to long-lasting emotional problems. Singer and actress Demi Lovato entered a rehabilitation center at age nineteen to receive medical treatment for eating disorders and other physical and emotional problems. She attributed some of her self-destructive behavior to low self-esteem that developed when she was teased and bullied

Singer Demi Lovato (pictured) entered a rehabilitation center at age nineteen to be treated for eating disorders. As a child, Lovato had been bullied about her weight.

because of her weight when she was nine years old. "Those girls never gave me an explanation for why they were bullying me," she said. "One of the words they called me was fat. At that age, you think, Oh, so I don't have friends because I'm fat."[23] Lovato struggled with anorexia, bulimia, and self-mutilation for many years before she finally sought treatment.

Peers are not always the source of teasing and bullying for overweight and obese children. Some children are made painfully aware of their weight issues by cruel comments from family members. "I have felt overweight since about three years old when my aunt said something bad about me and I realized that I was fat,"[24] commented Lola, age ten, in the book *Overweight: What Kids Say*. Whatever the source of the criticism, negative comments about a child's weight break down the child's self-esteem, which can in turn lead to deeper physical and emotional problems.

Online Resources Can Help

The Internet is an important source of information and support for overweight and obese children. Many young people find it helpful to interact with one another online in order to share stories and build a sense of community. Knowing that they are not alone in dealing with weight problems helps children and teens cope with the negative reactions they sometimes encounter from others.

Weigh2Rock is a popular Internet site where overweight kids come together online to support one another and get information on nutrition, exercise, and other weight-related topics. Robert Pretlow, a pediatrician who is involved in the care of overweight children and teens, created it with the purpose of giving overweight and obese kids a place where they could share their experiences, discuss the problems associated with being overweight, and find a source of encouragement. Over the years, thousands of children have posted to the Weigh2Rock site or used it to obtain information and support from other kids.

Many teens and preteens use the site as a forum to discuss how they became overweight and why it is so difficult for them to lose weight. One fourteen-year-old girl explained that her weight problems grew out of her home environment, which did not encourage healthy habits. "We have chips and stuff in the house that my dad likes to eat," she posted. "My mom usually cooks like fattier foods that I don't need. . . . They're not very active. My mom is busy a lot and my dad has an office job. . . . My question is this. Why can't they start living healthier . . . for me?"[25]

Other teens who post to the site share inspiring stories about their own efforts to lose weight and build healthier

From Chunky to Homebound

Billy was overweight as a small child, but his mother, Barbara, always thought he would outgrow it. "In kindergarten, he was a little chunky, and I used to tell everybody, 'Oh yeah, he's going to be my football player,'" she recalled. Over the years, though, Billy's weight gain only accelerated. By 2009 he was eighteen years old and weighed 800 pounds (363kg). He could not even leave his parents' house due to difficulties standing up and walking. He spent his days watching television and eating.

Although doctors had told Barbara for years that she needed to change Billy's eating habits, she failed to do so. Finally, Billy's health situation became so dire that doctors warned he might not live to see his twentieth birthday if he did not take drastic measures to lose weight. Billy underwent surgery to remove 70 pounds (32kg) of fat from his abdomen. He also had a procedure to remove 80 percent of his stomach. Following the surgeries, Barbara and Billy worked together to change his eating habits. He has since lost more than 300 pounds (136kg) and finds it much easier to move around. "When you see people in a situation like that, a lot of people snicker and make judgments," Billy said of being obese. "Don't judge a person by that, because there's a lot of roads that lead to where I was. [If you're] making them feel bad about themselves and making fun of them, you're just making them feel horrible. [It] never, never makes the situation any better."

"Understanding Obesity." Oprah.com, March 26, 2009. www.oprah.com/oprah show/Treating-Teen-Obesity/1#ixzz1V7psKPD9.

lives for themselves. Many of those who have successfully battled weight issues describe families that support them with encouragement and positive reinforcement. "I told my mom I wanted to try losing weight, and she supported me and asked me what kinds of foods she should buy at the grocery store," wrote an eighteen-year-old girl who weighed nearly 200 pounds (90kg). "Whenever I lose a single pound she's always proud of me."[26]

An early diagnosis of a child's obesity—and acceptance rather than denial of that diagnosis by parents—is an important factor in helping the child achieve a healthy weight. Families with obese members should also strive to recognize excess weight as a health issue rather than an appearance issue, and to create and nurture a positive emotional environment for children trying to lose weight. Finally, a child's capacity to make lasting changes to his or her diet and exercise routine often depends on the willingness of *all* members of the family to accept lifestyle changes.

CHAPTER 3

Endangering Lives

Medical professionals emphasize that childhood obesity is not just an appearance issue, it is a health issue. Obesity causes physical, emotional, and social harm to children. Unless parents and doctors help overweight and obese children change their eating and exercise habits, they run an increased risk of experiencing serious health problems for the rest of their lives.

Obesity-Related Diseases

One of the most dangerous aspects of childhood obesity is that it can contribute to other medical problems, including heart disease, high blood pressure, high cholesterol, and diabetes. Typically people do not develop these conditions until they are older adults. Childhood obesity can speed up the process, however, and increase people's risk of experiencing these medical issues at younger ages. Studies have found that these types of health problems are increasing in children, and experts associate this trend with the increase in childhood obesity.

The *Journal of the American Medical Association* published a study in 2007 about the link between obesity and hypertension (high blood pressure) in children. High blood pressure increases the risk of heart attacks, heart failure, and blocked arteries. The study evaluated 14,187 children and adolescents and found that 3.6 percent of them had hypertension. Among children who were overweight, however, 30 percent had high blood pressure. "Hypertension in children has been shown to correlate with family history of hypertension, low birth weight, and excess weight," the authors of the study stated. "With the increasing prevalence of childhood weight problems, increased attention to weight-related health conditions including hypertension is warranted. Several lines of evidence suggest that blood pressure in U.S. children and adolescents is increasing in parallel with weight."[27]

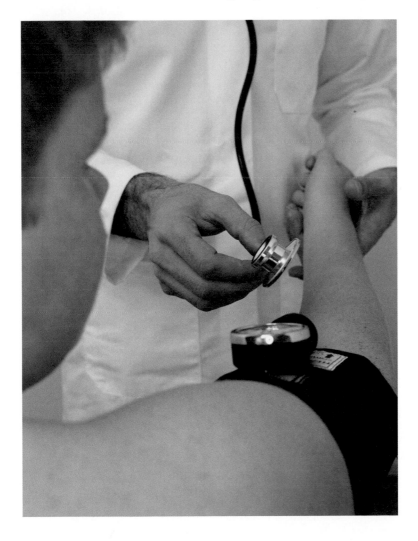

Obesity in children has been linked to hypertension, or high blood pressure, which increases the risk of heart attack.

Another dangerous disease linked to obesity is type 2 diabetes. Type 2 diabetes affects the body's ability to produce or use insulin, a hormone that is needed to allow the body to turn sugar from food into energy. Without enough insulin, sugar can accumulate in the bloodstream and create serious health problems. Diabetes complications can include heart disease, stroke, kidney disease, nerve damage, poor circulation, and blindness.

The number of children with type 2 diabetes (formerly known as adult-onset diabetes) doubled in the United States between 2005 and 2008. Much of this increase can be attributed to rising rates of childhood obesity. Obese children are twice as likely to develop type 2 diabetes as children who maintain a healthy weight. A 2006 study by the University of Michigan found that diabetes affected more than 229,000 Americans under the age of eighteen, and that one-third of the children and adolescents diagnosed with diabetes were obese. Younger people are also more likely to experience health complications related to diabetes. For instance, children and teens diagnosed with type 2 diabetes are five times more likely to develop kidney disease than people who develop diabetes as adults.

Multiple Health Problems

Obese children have an increased likelihood of developing several other health problems that are usually associated with adults. For instance, obese children often develop high cholesterol levels in the bloodstream. High cholesterol can contribute to the buildup of fatty deposits called plaques in the arteries. These plaques can cause arteries to narrow and harden, which can lead to a heart attack or stroke later in life.

A 2008 American Heart Association study found that obese children have as much plaque in their neck arteries as middle-aged adults. Doctors used ultrasound tests to measure the plaque buildup in the carotid arteries of seventy obese children and teens with an average age of thirteen. The researchers found that the average carotid artery intima-media thickness (CIMT) in these young people was .018 inches (.45mm), which is typical of adults in their mid-forties. This buildup of fatty deposits in the neck arteries places the kids at high risk for developing heart disease and other health problems that do not typically occur in children. "My premonition is that we will see more premature angina [severe chest pain due to poor blood supply to the heart muscle] and strokes and such,"[28] concluded study author Geetha Raghuveer, an associate professor of pediatrics at the University of Missouri–Kansas City School of Medicine.

Several other health hazards can result from childhood obesity as well. An obese child's extra weight can create problems with the development of his or her lungs, for instance, resulting in asthma or other breathing problems. Another common health risk for obese children is sleep apnea. This

A young boy is treated for problems related to morbid obesity. This condition increases the chance of developing other health problems, including respiratory difficulties.

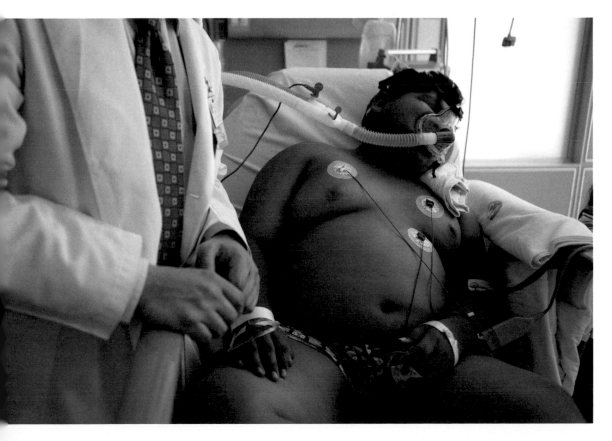

disorder occurs when a person's breathing is abnormal or disrupted while he or she is asleep. Symptoms of sleep apnea include loud snoring, shallow breathing, or lengthy pauses in breathing during sleep, as well as excessive daytime drowsiness. These breathing problems interfere with sleep patterns and contribute to other health risks, including cardiovascular, behavioral, and psychiatric complications. Obese children and adults are at a greater risk of developing obstructive sleep apnea because fat deposits in the neck area can narrow air passageways and interfere with breathing.

Medical researchers, doctors, and public health experts agree that these trends are deeply alarming. "Because of the increasing rates of obesity, unhealthy eating habits and physical inactivity," declared former U.S. surgeon general Richard Carmona, "we may see the first generation that will be less healthy and have a shorter life expectancy than their parents."[29]

Adult Obesity Probability

Childhood obesity has so many lasting health effects in part because obese children have a high probability of becoming obese adults. A 2011 study by the Centers for Disease Control and Prevention (CDC) found that a preschool-age child who is obese has an approximate 30 percent chance of being obese as an adult. Additionally, the CDC found that 80 percent of adolescents who were obese between the ages of ten and fifteen continued to be obese at age twenty-five. One reason for this trend is that the eating and exercise habits people develop in childhood usually remain the same into adulthood. Another factor is that once fat cells develop, they are never lost. If a person loses weight, the fat cells decrease in size but remain in the body, making it easier for that person to regain weight.

As the rate of childhood obesity grows, so does the percentage of the adult population that is overweight or obese. A 2007 study published in the *New England Journal of Medicine* used data on childhood obesity rates to estimate that by 2020, as many as 44 percent of American women and 37 percent of American men will be obese at age thirty-five. The authors

Advice for Parents

At the age of fourteen, Taylor LeBaron weighed 297 pounds (135kg). After losing 150 pounds (68kg), Taylor wrote a book about his experiences called *Cutting Myself in Half*. He recounts how being obese as a child was frightening for him, especially because he was too embarrassed to share his feelings with his family and ask for help.

Taylor's book mentions a number of things he wishes he had told his family. For instance, he felt terrified of developing weight-related diseases like diabetes. Although he often pretended that his obesity did not bother him, he wanted desperately to attain a healthy weight. Taylor also worried about not fitting in with other kids his age. "My weight placed a huge barrier between me and my thin peers," he acknowledged. "The more isolated I felt, the more I turned to food for comfort. And the more I turned to food, the bigger and more isolated I became."

Even though Taylor usually laughed along with kids who made fun of his weight, he admitted that he felt deeply hurt by the teasing he endured. He also blamed himself for being overweight and felt miserable and hopeless when he thought about how much weight he needed to lose. Finally, Taylor wished his family had tried harder to talk to him about his weight problem. "I was terrified and knew I needed help. I was also self-conscious and embarrassed," he recalled. "But I would have listened—eventually—if my family had approached me about my weight."

Taylor LeBaron. "Super-Sized Advice from a Former Fat Kid." *Huffington Post*, March 11, 2010. www.huffington post.com/taylor-lebaron/super-sized-advice-from-a_b _493960.html#s73430.

also predicted that the prevalence of heart disease will rise by as much as 16 percent and heart disease deaths by as much as 19 percent for Americans between the ages of thirty-five and fifty. In other words, researchers believe that obesity will produce one hundred thousand additional heart disease deaths each year among people in this age group by 2020.

Emotional and Academic Consequences of Obesity

In addition to the many physical diseases and disorders that can result from childhood obesity, there are a number of potential psychological and emotional consequences as well. One of the main consequences of obesity is low self-esteem, which in turn can lead to eating disorders, poor academic performance, depression, and other issues.

Many studies have found a link between children being overweight or obese and having a poor self-image. A study by the Children's Defense Fund found that boys ages nine to sixteen who were chronically obese were significantly more likely to have depression than peers who were not overweight or obese. Another study, published in *Applied Developmen-*

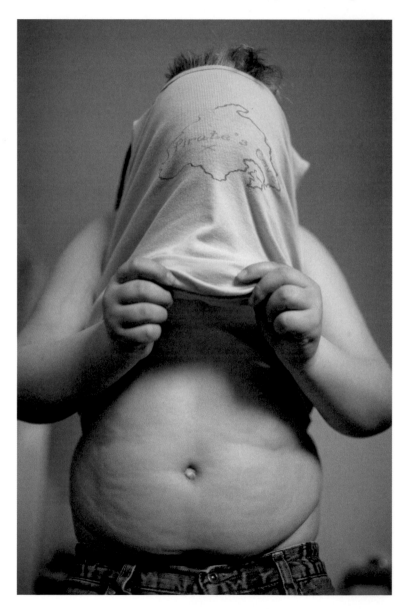

Studies have found a link between obesity and poor self-image.

tal Science in 2010, followed about eight thousand children from kindergarten through the third grade. Children who were overweight in the third grade reported less favorable relationships with peers and also felt unpopular. Similarly, kindergarteners with weight problems were more likely to feel sad, lonely, and worried than their classmates who were a healthy weight. These feelings increased as the children entered higher grades. "Overweight and obesity are terribly stigmatizing conditions [subject to public disapproval], regardless of age," said Sara Gable of the University of Missouri, Columbia. "Living as a member of a stigmatized group is stressful and can produce feelings of anxiety, depression, and loneliness."[30]

Obese and overweight children are also more likely to struggle in school. A 2005 study by the California Department of Education found a correlation between fitness scores that included body mass index (BMI) percentages and academic test scores. Kids who were deemed fit (by standard tests of aerobic capacity, BMI, abdominal strength, trunk strength, upper-body strength, and overall flexibility) scored twice as high on academic tests as those who were deemed unfit.

Charles Hillman, an associate professor of kinesiology at the University of Illinois, reported similar findings in a 2007 study of 259 third- and fifth-grade students in Illinois. Hillman's research showed that BMI and aerobic capacity had a much stronger influence on academic scores than the other four fitness factors. Hillman continued his study using two groups of twenty students, one fit and the other unfit. He gave each group a series of cognitive tests of attention, working memory, and processing speed while measuring the electrical activity in their brains using an electroencephalogram (EEG). The fit children showed more activity in the prefrontal cortex, an area of the brain known for its control over other brain processes, than the unfit children.

Two other studies published in 2008 by Professor John R. Slate and his team at Sam Houston State University had similar results. Slate found that students whose body mass indexes were in the obese category were more likely to do poorly in teacher-assigned grading as well as in state-administered testing. These results held true across all racial and ethnic groups.

The authors attributed some of the decline in obese students' academic performance to poor attendance. The Children's Defense Fund reported that children who were overweight or obese had rates of school absenteeism that were 20 percent higher than those of their classmates who were a healthy weight. In addition, overweight or obese children were significantly more likely to miss more than two weeks of school in an academic year and to repeat a grade in school.

High Risk of Eating Disorders

Losing weight is a key factor in improving or preventing many of the physical and emotional problems that can affect overweight and obese children and teens. Weight loss must be achieved in a healthy manner, however, or else it can create even more problems. In their desperation to lose weight, many obese young people—particularly teens—try extreme dieting methods, including fad diets, fasting, and laxatives (foods or medications taken to promote bowel movements). All of these weight-loss methods can be dangerous to their long-term health. Most worrisome is that extreme dieting methods can lead to the development of eating disorders. According to the National Eating Disorders Association, as many as 10 million American women and 1 million American men are affected by an eating disorder.

One of the most common eating disorders among obese teenagers is bulimia. A person with bulimia will typically go through cycles of bingeing (eating large quantities of food in a short period of time) and purging (trying to get rid of the calories consumed, usually by self-induced vomiting or by taking laxatives). According to pediatrician Robert Pretlow, about 15 percent of overweight kids demonstrate bulimic behavior. The condition is much more common in girls than boys. Bulimia can cause a number of serious health complications, including tooth decay,

FOOD FACT

According to 2010 data compiled by the Centers for Disease Control and Prevention, the state with the highest obesity rate is Mississippi, where 34 percent of the population is classified as obese. The state with the lowest obesity rate is Colorado, at 21 percent.

dehydration, electrolyte imbalance, irregular heartbeat, acid reflux, and damage to the esophagus or colon.

Another common eating disorder is anorexia. People with anorexia develop a distorted body image and an intense fear of gaining weight. They severely limit the amount of food they eat and may exercise excessively in an effort to burn calories. British reality-TV star Nikki Grahame has battled anorexia since she was eight years old and has been institutionalized for treatment eleven different times. "I have this phobia of having more than 400 calories at any one time," she admitted. "I can't allow myself to sleep if I feel I haven't done enough exercise. I don't sit down for two hours after I've eaten."[31] Like bulimia, anorexia is most common among young women. It is a serious mental health disorder that

Bulimia is an eating disorder in which an individual rapidly consumes large quantities of food (bingeing) and then induces vomiting (purging) to get rid of the huge caloric intake.

can have life-threatening complications, including anemia, bone loss, electrolyte imbalance, heart problems, kidney problems, and starvation.

There are other types of eating disorders as well. Exercise addiction, for example, occurs when a person becomes obsessed with exercise and works out for multiple hours each day, often disregarding other important life events in order to exercise. Like other eating disorders, it can cause both physical and psychological harm.

Often subjected to ridicule and bullying, obese children are more likely to feel depressed, lonely, and anxious.

Targeted by Bullies

Being teased and bullied is a common occurrence for children and teenagers who are overweight or obese. A 2007 study published in the *Journal of Pediatric Psychology* dis-

cussed the effects of bullying on one hundred children who were overweight or at risk for being overweight. About one-quarter of the children reported having significant problems with bullies during the two weeks prior to being questioned. The results indicated that the bullied kids were more likely to feel depressed, lonely, and anxious.

The study also found that bullying often caused kids to avoid playgrounds, gym class, and sports teams, all of which provide opportunities to improve physical fitness. "When you think about it, it makes intuitive sense, when you consider the hallmark signs of depression—sadness, fatigue, lack of interest in things you used to like," said study author Eric Storch of the University of South Florida. "When kids are having a tough time with peers, and struggling with depression, then this can translate to reduced rates of physical activity."[32]

Dating and Other Social Activities

For obese teens, social situations often cause extreme anxiety. One particular area that results in anxious feelings is dating. Many obese teens have low self-esteem and believe that no one will want to date them because of their weight. If they do go out on a date, poor self-image may prevent them from enjoying themselves.

Another risk is that overweight or obese teens may become sexually active in a quest to gain affection and feel wanted. According to pediatrician Michael Rich of Children's Hospital Boston, weight problems can make teenage girls vulnerable to sexual exploitation. "They are perceived as being older and more mature than they truly are. That they are easy," he explained. "That they are more willing to trade sex for affection than somebody who everybody wants because she looks like the front cover of a magazine."[33]

Other obese teens avoid the pressure of dating and other social activities by isolating themselves. To eliminate potential sources of teasing or bullying, they do not engage in any social activities. They then turn to food for comfort. This cycle can result in even more weight gain and lower self-esteem.

Overweight and Happy

American society is full of messages that suggest that people who are fit and slim are happier than individuals who are overweight and obese. The television, film, and music industries all suggest that fit and slim physiques are the ideal, and doctors and scientists regularly warn us about the physical, emotional, and economic problems that often come with the extra pounds. It is worth noting, however, that according to many overweight people, they not miserable. They are happy and content and lead interesting and rewarding lives.

Girls and women feel particularly intense pressure to be thin, but according to Lisa Colles, who debated fellow writer Kia Hansen on the topic in a British newspaper, it can be liberating to reject that pressure. "In our body-obsessed society it's not easy to be overweight and happy—but it's certainly possible," said Colles. "For many women it's not so much being fat that causes unhappiness, but the message that they are unacceptable, the relentless pressure to be thin, and the constant dieting and anxiety that accompanies that. . . . We are quite simply not all meant to be the same, and it's time to celebrate and embrace diversity. . . . Why can't we all just be accepted as we are?"

Hansen agrees that "being overweight isn't automatically going to make you miserable, just as losing weight isn't a guaranteed path to happiness." Hansen believes, though, that the issue is more complex than that:

> People who aren't happy being overweight aren't saying there's anything socially unacceptable about being fat—they are just saying it's unacceptable for them personally. Losing weight for these people is about more than image; it's about taking back control of their lives and gaining some self respect. . . . The real question shouldn't be, "can you be fat and happy?" but "are you?"

Kia Hansen and Lisa Colles. "Debate: Can You Be Fat and Happy, or Are the 'Big is Beautiful' Lobby Fooling Themselves?" *Independent (London)*, October 18, 1998. www.independent.co.uk/life-style/debate-can-you-be-fat-and-happy-or-are-the-big-is-beautiful-lobby-fooling-themselves-1178987.html.

Although a source of the unhappiness experienced by overweight girls is the message that they are unacceptable in a society that values thinness, experts believe it is not impossible to be overweight and happy.

Significant Economic Costs

Obesity is not only costly in terms of physical and emotional health. It also can take a heavy economic toll on individuals and families. There are a number of medical costs associated with obesity, including treatment of chronic health conditions like diabetes and high blood pressure. The annual costs for prescription drugs, emergency room treatment, and outpatient services related to childhood obesity total more than $14 billion in the United States, with an additional $238 million in inpatient hospital costs. According to the CDC, 9 percent of all U.S. medical costs in 2008 were related to obesity.

The cost of treating a child's obesity and associated health problems is also expensive on a personal level. A 2006 study

Annual Cost of Obesity

This bar chart compares the annual medical cost of obesity in the United States in 1998 and 2008.

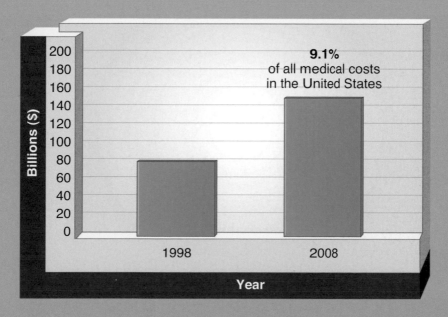

Taken from: Cynthia L. Ogden. "Childhood Obesity in the United States: The Magnitude of the Problem." www.cdc.gov /about/grand-rounds/archives/2010/download/GR-062010.pdf, page 16.

by the Thomson Corporation and Medstat found that a child treated for obesity and related conditions is roughly three times more expensive for the health care system than an average child. The same study found that obese children are two to three times more likely to be hospitalized than those who maintain a healthy weight. Obese children are also more likely to be diagnosed with mental health, joint, and bone disorders than other children.

All of the costs of childhood obesity—physical, emotional, social, and monetary—are great. Furthermore, since obese children run a high risk of becoming obese adults, those costs are likely to last a lifetime.

CHAPTER 4

Reclaiming Health

C hildhood obesity is a health issue that can be overcome with commitment and hard work, experts say. The entire family must be dedicated to making important changes in their daily nutrition and exercise habits. If parents, children, and pediatricians work together, they can develop a program of options that will give overweight and obese children their best chance at living a healthy life.

Making Lifestyle Changes

Experts agree that there is no quick and easy fix for obesity. Fad diets, diet pills, excessive exercise, and other sorts of extreme actions do not work over the long term. The only way to truly overcome obesity, according to health professionals, is to develop and maintain healthy eating and exercise habits. These habits need to be incorporated into a child's daily routine. "The best way to lose weight is to make long-term changes in the way you eat—changes you can live with for the rest of your life," stated renowned health and spiritual adviser Deepak Chopra. "There are many ways to do this. You can limit calories or portion sizes, or you may choose to limit certain foods (the unhealthy, fattening ones!) and emphasize others."[34]

Another vital component to improving the health of overweight and obese children is getting the entire family involved in the process. "The key to helping your child beat obesity is to develop healthier habits for your whole family. Your child will not succeed at losing weight if he is munching carrot sticks while everyone else slurps chocolate milk shakes!" noted the More4Kids website. "In addition, change your habits slowly so that everyone has time to adjust to the new routines."[35] The healthy habits recommended by the website include exercising for sixty minutes and eating five servings of fruits and vegetables each day.

Studies support the idea that parental involvement helps overweight and obese children succeed in attaining a healthy weight. A 2010 Australian study had parents of overweight or obese children take a six-month-long healthy lifestyle course. The course emphasized reducing portion sizes, reading nutrition labels, being a good role model, and setting limits. Parents used the information to assess their own eating patterns and set their own goals for change. Some of the lifestyle changes included limiting TV to no more than two hours per day and scheduling more active family activities. The parents also committed to making small dietary changes, such as eating more fruits and vegetables, using reduced-fat dairy products, and drinking fewer sweetened beverages. By the end of the six-month course, their children's body mass index (BMI) and waist circumference had dropped by an average of 10 percent. When the investigators followed up with the families eighteen months later, they found that the children had kept the weight off.

How to Change?

Recognizing the need to make lifestyle changes is only the first step toward improving the health of an overweight or obese child. Deciding on the best way to make those changes is the next step. In some cases, professionals can be valuable in helping families develop a plan that they can stick with over the long term. Nutritionists, for example, can help families learn to make healthy changes in their eating habits. A nutritionist can assess a family's typical diet and determine the areas in which changes should be made.

Many times people think they are making healthy choices when in fact they are not. One example of an unhealthy choice people often make is deciding to drink diet sodas and eat fat-free snacks when they are trying to lose weight. The problem with these choices is that they have little or no nutritional value and contain artificial sweeteners that can actually serve to increase appetite. "Fat-free processed foods and snacks will always make you eat too much, encourage sugar cravings, and keep you unsatisfied,"[36] reported Annemarie Colbin, founder of the Natural Gourmet Institute for Health and Culinary Arts.

FOOD FACT

In a 2009 survey, 10.6 percent of American high school students reported not eating for twenty-four hours or more during the previous thirty days in an effort to lose weight or to keep from gaining weight.

Rather than being healthy choices, diet sodas and fat-free snacks have little nutritive value and are often loaded with artifical sweeteners, known to increase appetite.

Similarly, some people think that skipping meals will help them lose weight because they will consume fewer calories. Experts say that this is another unhealthy choice, especially when people choose to skip breakfast. Most people who skip meals get so hungry that they consume more calories at the next meal than they otherwise would have. In addition, skipping meals can prevent people from getting all of the nutrients they need. Studies show that people who eat a healthy breakfast actually tend to consume fewer calories through-out the day and find it easier to maintain a healthy weight.

Changing a Family's Eating Habits

After having three children, Kristi Kingston gradually adopted poor eating habits and began struggling to control her weight. She soon realized that her choices were affecting her children's health as well. "In the midst of my own struggle, I noticed last fall that my nine-year-old son had put on more weight around his middle," wrote Kingston. "It wasn't hard to pinpoint the problem: poor food choices. My kids would eat a bag of chips as a replacement for a meal while watching TV or playing games on the laptop."[37]

Kingston became concerned about the future health problems her children might face as a result of their poor eating habits and unhealthy weight, especially because her family had a history of diabetes, high blood pressure, and high cholesterol. She worried that unless she changed how the family ate, she and her children were headed down the same path. "I wasn't looking for a quick fix but rather a healthy approach to eating. My overall goal was to teach my children to make good choices, including snacks. I wanted 'bad' foods to be something they enjoyed on rare occasions as opposed to several times a day," she explained on her blog. "I also wanted to teach them a way of eating that they could carry with them through their lives, not a 'diet' they would follow until they reached some magical goal weight."[38]

As part of the changes, the Kingston family got rid of chips, candy, and other processed snacks and replaced them with dried fruits and nuts. Kingston also made sure that fresh fruit was always readily available in bowls on the kitchen table. The children soon discovered that they liked healthy foods such as boiled eggs, yogurt, and fresh vegetables. The family found it easy to continue these lifestyle changes and has become healthier and more fit as a result.

Weight-Loss Camps

Another option for obese children and teens seeking to make healthy lifestyle changes is a weight-loss camp. Health professionals only recommend camps that provide information and

"I Used to Be Fat"

Obesity and weight loss have become popular topics on television shows such as *The Biggest Loser, Extreme Makeover: Weight Loss Edition,* and *DietTribe.* In 2011 MTV launched a new reality series aimed at younger viewers called *I Used to Be Fat.* Each episode follows a severely overweight or obese teenager as he or she tries to lose a significant amount of weight over the three-month period between graduating from high school and starting college. Each teen receives intensive physical training and individualized nutrition advice from a personal trainer. One episode followed a teen named Makenzie during the summer after her high school graduation. During the course of her summer training she went from 273 pounds (124kg) down to 224 pounds (102kg). Another teen, Gabriella, lost 90 pounds (41kg) during the course of the show.

Some people criticize the series for showing teens using excessive means, such as exercising several hours a day, to lose weight. They argue that such methods are not sustainable over the long run for most teens. But fans claim that the show inspires other overweight teens to make needed changes in their lives. They also appreciate the show's emphasis on exercise and nutritious-eating habits. Gabriella says that appearing on the show changed her life. "I lost weight the only way to really lose weight, by eating right and exercising," she says. "I had a great support system. I had my family and friends but most importantly, I had my amazing trainer, Katie. I owe her my life."

"Meet Gabriella of MTV's 'I Used to Be Fat.'" *Seventeen,* December 22, 2010. www.seventeen.com/cosmogirl/mtv-i-used-to-be-fat-interview.

Potential contestants for The Biggest Loser *TV show fill out applications for a chance to appear on the program, where participants compete to lose the most weight.*

support to help attendees make lasting lifestyle changes and improve their overall health. They do not recommend camps that encourage obese teenagers to lose weight as quickly as possible. "The camps vary in the services they provide and the philosophies they stand by. Thus, the decision to send a teen to a particular camp should be taken seriously," stated the Livestrong website. "The better camps educate teens on what healthy eating is and why it is important. Camps should also encourage physical activity. When possible, choose a camp that offers healthy body image and self-esteem building skills as well."[39]

Wellspring is a national provider of weight-loss camps that offer programs for kids, teens, and families. Wellspring camps emphasize a scientific approach to diet and activity management in order to help campers make lasting changes to their lifestyles. According to the organization's website, Wellspring provides services to more than one thousand families per year, and 70 percent of its campers either maintain their weight or continue losing weight after they return home. "Whereas our goal is to teach kids to love and adopt an active, healthy lifestyle, fat camps force kids to exercise and eat very restricted diets. The result is that kids leave fat camps relieved to return to their previous habits, often regaining all of the weight lost at camp," states the Wellspring website. "We understand that excess weight can affect all aspects of an individual's health and happiness, and that losing weight requires change on many levels."[40]

The main downside of weight-loss camps is that they are typically costly. Health insurance plans do not always cover such programs, either. For families that can afford it, though, the tuition can be a wise investment. The right weight-loss camp can yield positive results that last a lifetime.

Jacqueline Hattar attended Camp Shane, a weight-loss camp in upstate New York, when she was fourteen years old. At the time, she weighed 285 pounds (84kg) and could not remember ever being a healthy weight. She had battled with self-image and weight issues for so long that she felt she needed to make major changes in her lifestyle. Jacqueline learned healthy eating and exercise habits at camp, and she incorporated those habits into her life after returning home.

"Exercise is now a big priority in my life, and I set the alarm early every morning to work out at the gym," she said. "And I avoid unhealthy temptations at the cafeteria. I always pack my own healthy lunch and snacks for school." Jacqueline's camp experience helped her attain a healthy weight, and she also gained self-esteem and confidence. "The biggest change I made in my life was my perception of myself," she stated. "In learning to accept myself, I now realize that outward changes cannot come without inward changes first."[41]

Exercise Is Key

For families who cannot afford a weight-loss camp, there are less expensive ways to improve the health of overweight and obese children and teens. One of the most important healthy habits to adopt is regular exercise. Exercise provides a wide range of physical and emotional health benefits for everyone in the family. There are several inexpensive options for families looking to establish a physical fitness routine.

Most YMCAs across the country, for instance, offer inexpensive family fitness programs. Many of these programs also include nutritional information and advice. The YMCA in Norfolk, Virginia, offers Y-Change classes for free with a family membership, which costs about $90 per month. The Y-Change program features nutrition and fitness education as well as group exercise sessions. A family membership also includes access to all the Y's exercise facilities and fitness classes.

One of the easiest ways for parents and children to incorporate physical fitness into their daily routines is to exercise together as a family. Fun outdoor family activities include biking, hiking, swimming, skiing, and playing various sports and games. The key is to get the whole family moving on a regular basis, with the goal of exercising sixty minutes per day. Some video games and workout DVDs provide indoor family exercise options. Families can play games such as *Wii Fit* or *Just Dance* together, or they can try workout DVDs that involve dancing,

FOOD FACT

Walking up the stairs rather than riding an elevator or escalator burns an extra nine calories per minute.

kickboxing, or yoga. Fitness experts point out that people are much more likely to stick with an exercise program if they can find something that they enjoy doing.

Andrew Berry convinced his family to join a gym in order to improve their overall health and help him lose weight. The eleven-year-old had grown tired of being teased by classmates for having chubby cheeks and a round belly. He told his parents that he wanted to adopt a healthier lifestyle. They not only supported his choice but decided to get in shape along with him. The Berry family joined Body Fit Las Vegas, a fitness club in their neighborhood that offers training for the whole family. Marcus Niemo, the club's owner, is committed to fighting childhood obesity by providing families with affordable gym access. "It's bringing parents and kids

Most YMCAs in the United States offer inexpensive family and youth fitness programs, including activities such as exercise classes, swimming, and hiking.

together," he explained. "As a parent, you have to be an example. Plus, it's bonding."[42]

Andrew works out with his older brother, Frederick, and his parents nearly every day. During the school year, the boys get up early in the morning to lift weights with their dad. Exercising together has become a habit, and it has made the entire family feel more fit and healthy. Although no one in the Berry family has stepped on a scale since joining the gym, they all say that they can see and feel the difference in their bodies. "I know I've lost a little weight," Andrew said. "I know I've gotten stronger. I feel better. It's helped me a lot."[43]

Weight-Loss Surgery

Exercise may be difficult or even dangerous for extremely obese young people, especially those who have diabetes, cardiovascular risk factors, joint pain, or other health problems related to obesity. In some cases, weight loss must occur before exercise becomes an option. Some people in this situation choose to undergo bariatric (weight-loss) surgery. Bariatric surgery usually enables people to lose a great deal of weight in a relatively short time, but it involves many potential risks and side effects. Health professionals generally do not recommend weight-loss surgery for adolescents and teenagers, but there are exceptions. Research indicates that about one thousand teenagers in the United States have some sort of bariatric surgery each year.

There are two main types of weight-loss surgery. In gastric band surgery, a surgeon places an adjustable silicone band (sometimes known as a lap band) around the upper part of the stomach. This band reduces the size of the stomach and limits the amount of food the person can eat without feeling sick. Gastric banding is considered the least-invasive and safest form of bariatric surgery. The procedure can be reversed if necessary, allowing the stomach to return to its normal size. A potential downside of this procedure is that some patients experience nausea and vomiting. These side effects can often be reduced by adjusting the tightness of the band. Other complications that can occur are wound infections, minor bleeding, pain, constipation, or diarrhea. The risk of death from gastric band surgery is one in two thousand patients.

The other main type of bariatric surgery is a gastric bypass procedure. Although there are different types of gastric bypass procedures, they all involve surgically reducing the size of the stomach by up to 90 percent and reconnecting the small intestine to the new stomach pouch. Roux en-Y is the most popular gastric bypass method in the United States. The surgeon staples the patient's stomach to create a small pouch, divides the small intestine into a Y-shape, and connects part of the small intestine to the stomach pouch to form a passage for nutrients to pass through.

Gastric bypass procedures enable patients to feel full after eating a limited amount of food. As a result, an average patient will lose 65 to 80 percent of his or her excess body

Extremely obese people may elect to undergo one of two types of bariatric (weight-loss) surgery. Using different methods, each is designed to restrict the amount of food that enters the stomach.

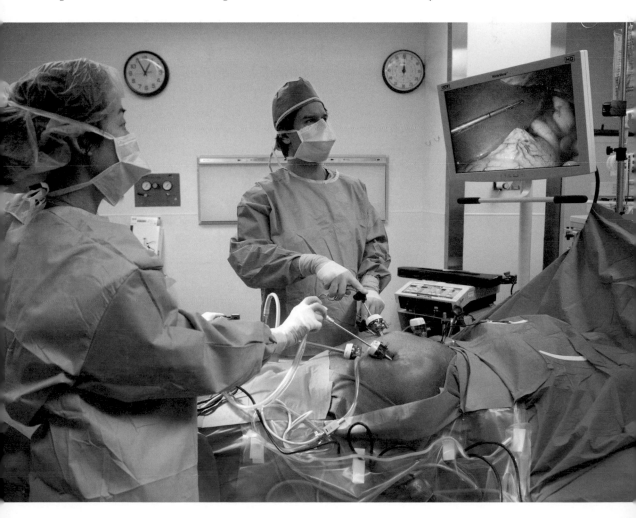

weight. Most patients also experience considerable relief from obesity-related health problems, such as diabetes, high blood pressure, and sleep apnea. Like all major surgeries, however, gastric bypass procedures involve risks. Possible complications include vitamin and mineral deficiencies, dehydration, gallstones, blood clots and, in rare cases, death.

Doctors generally recommend bariatric surgery only for adult patients who are morbidly obese, meaning that their BMI is greater than 40. They sometimes also approve surgery for adults with a BMIs between 35 and 40 who also have serious health problems related to obesity. In these cases, the potentially lifesaving health benefits of surgery outweigh the risks. Weight-loss surgery is rarely recommended for people under the age of eighteen unless they are morbidly obese, have severe obesity-related medical conditions, and have tried unsuccessfully to achieve a healthy weight through various diet and exercise programs. Doctors also typically will not perform the surgery on children until they have gone through puberty and have stopped growing. They worry that the increased risk of vitamin deficiencies after surgery might affect bone growth or sexual maturation. In addition to the risks involved, bariatric surgery is not usually considered appropriate for young patients because it can be difficult for them to follow postoperative dietary restrictions.

A Successful Surgery

Shaina had bariatric surgery in 2011 at the age of sixteen. At the time, she weighed 242 pounds (110kg) and had developed a number of obesity-related health problems. The most serious of these health issues was a buildup of pressure inside her skull, which was damaging her optic nerve and affecting her vision. Doctors told Shaina and her family that she needed to lose weight quickly to reduce the pressure or else the damage to her eyesight would become irreversible. Three months after her surgery, Shaina had lost 58 pounds (26kg) and had gone from a size twenty to a twelve.

Although Shaina is happy with the results, she and other teens who have undergone weight-loss surgery often have

Do Diet Pills Work?

Go from a size sixteen to a size eight in a month! Lose weight while you sleep! These are just some of the promises made in advertisements for diet pills. Over-the-counter diet pills—those that can be purchased without a doctor's prescription—can lure overweight teenagers with their promises of quick results. According to health professionals, though, diet pills are often ineffective and can even be dangerous. Products marketed as nutritional supplements or weight-loss aids are not subject to the same rigorous tests and safety standards as prescription drugs, so there is little evidence to support the miraculous claims of their manufacturers.

Prescription weight-loss drugs are also not a good option for children. There are a few prescription weight-loss medications, such as orlistat and sibutramine, that have been found to be safe and effective for adults when combined with a healthy diet and exercise program. But the U.S. Food and Drug Administration (FDA) has not approved these drugs for use by children younger than sixteen years of age. Since children's bodies are smaller and more susceptible to drug toxicity than those of adults, it is more difficult to determine a safe dosage of medication. In addition, some diet

According to health experts, diet pills are often ineffective, and some may even be harmful.

pills work by preventing the body from absorbing fat, which also interferes with the absorption of fat-soluble vitamins. These vitamins are important for growth and development during childhood and adolescence.

difficulty dealing with the side effects. Shaina can only eat soft food or food that has been mashed up, and she must take a daily multivitamin to prevent nutritional deficiencies. Michelle Montani, who underwent weight-loss surgery at age fifteen when she weighed 250 pounds (113kg), also had trouble adjusting to her new diet. "My body was different day to day," she recalls. "One day I could tolerate mac and cheese; the next day I was throwing up. It's a really hard transition. . . . You have to retrain your body how to eat."[44] Montani says that the overall improvement in her health was worth the difficulties she experienced. By 2011, at age nineteen, she had lost 110 pounds (50kg). Like others who have undergone bariatric surgery, however, she emphasizes that it should not be considered a quick fix for obesity. Patients still must exercise regularly and eat balanced meals in order to maintain a healthy weight.

CHAPTER **5**

A Revolution Against Obesity

Childhood obesity is increasingly being recognized as a global problem. Countries around the world are concerned that obesity is creating a wide range of health problems that have serious economic consequences, from decreased worker productivity to increased health care costs. Initiatives are under way throughout the world aimed at changing people's lifestyles in order to promote good health.

Obesity's Impact on the National Economy

The strength of a nation's economy depends on the productivity of its people. When workers battle health problems related to obesity, their productivity declines. A study published in the *Journal of Occupational and Environmental Medicine* found that reduced work productivity due to obesity costs the United States an estimated $28.7 billion annually. People who are obese also tend to miss more days of work and to be restricted in their activities at work due to health problems. Absenteeism due to obesity and related health complications costs the United States more than $4.3 billion annually.

Reduced work productivity due to obesity costs the United States $28.7 billion annually.

Rising rates of obesity have also led to significant increases in the nation's overall health care costs. In 1998 the United States spent an estimated $74.2 billion, or 5.3 percent of all medical spending nationwide, on health issues related to obesity. By 2006 obesity-related health care costs had increased to $147 billion, or 9.1 percent of the nation's annual medical spending. As obesity rates continue to rise, the associated health care costs are likely to grow too.

Let's Move

Childhood obesity has received attention from the highest levels of the U.S. government in recent years. In February 2010 the White House initiated the Let's Move program, which is specifically dedicated to improving the health and fitness of young Americans. First Lady Michelle Obama heads this program. "We want to eliminate this problem of childhood obesity in a generation. We want to get that done,"

Obama explained. "We want our kids to face a different and more optimistic future in terms of their lifespan."[45]

To launch the Let's Move initiative, President Barack Obama created the first-ever Task Force on Childhood Obesity to review all federal programs and policies relating to child nutrition and physical activity and develop a national action plan. The action plan aims to reduce the U.S. childhood obesity rate to just 5 percent by 2030—the same rate as in the late 1970s, before childhood obesity rates began to rise. To achieve its goals, the plan focuses on increasing physical activity, empowering parents with the tools and knowledge to raise healthy children, and providing healthy food in schools.

Let's Move has launched several programs designed to boost the nutritional value of school lunches. It obtained commitments from three of the nation's largest food-service providers to ensure that school lunch menus meet recommended levels of fat, sugar, and whole grains within five years. The companies also agreed to double the amount of fruits and vegetables served within ten years. In addition, a coalition made up of the Fruit and Vegetable Alliance; the Food, Family, and Farming Foundation; and the United Fresh Produce Association committed to installing six thousand salad bars in schools across the country within three years. Another Let's Move initiative, called the Chefs Move to Schools program, involves nearly two thousand chefs who have volunteered to visit schools and help educate kids about making healthy food choices. The chefs also work within the school community to help create healthier school lunch menus.

Let's Move has also launched many programs to encourage children's physical fitness. Let's Move teamed up with Disney, the National Hockey League, and Major League Baseball to create a series of public service announcements that encourage children and their families to exercise. These announcements, which have appeared on television, radio, and billboards nationwide,

FOOD FACT

More than 70 percent of the milk distributed in school cafeterias is flavored, according to the Milk Processor Education Program.

AMERICA'S MOVE TO RAISE A
HEALTHIER GENERATION C...

First Lady Michelle Obama speaks about her Let's Move initiative at a Pennsylvania elementary school. Her program has developed a national action plan to fight obesity.

feature famous actors and athletes urging children to play sports and be active.

Other U.S. Anti-Obesity Initiatives

The federal government's efforts to combat childhood obesity also include new and updated laws. In 2010, for example, President Obama signed the Healthy, Hunger-Free Kids Act into law. This legislation authorizes $4.5 billion in federal funding over ten years for school meal and child nutrition programs for low-income children. According to former U.S. senator Bill Frist, vice chairman of the Partnership for a Healthier America, "this bi-partisan legislation will significantly enhance the quality of food for our children for generations to come and is a dramatic step forward in reducing childhood obesity. As a physician, I know smart nutrition leads to healthy and productive lives."[46]

The U.S. Centers for Disease Control and Prevention (CDC) is responsible for directing another federal project aimed at combating childhood obesity in low-income families. The CDC's four-year Childhood Obesity Demonstration Project, which was launched in 2011, uses a number of innovative approaches to encourage children ages two to twelve to eat a healthy diet and be physically active. It works with existing community partners—such as schools, daycare centers, parks and recreation programs, and grocery stores—to support programs that improve child nutrition and promote physical fitness. It also employs community health workers to inform and educate hard-to-reach populations (such as families with limited English proficiency) about nutrition, obesity prevention, health insurance enrollment opportunities, and disease management.

President Barack Obama signs the Healthy, Hunger-Free Kids Act on December 13, 2010. The law authorizes $4.5 billion in funding for school meals and child nutrition programs for low-income children.

Changing the Food Pyramid

For twenty years, the U.S. Department of Agriculture (USDA) used the Food Guide Pyramid as a visual aid to teach people about healthy eating. The Food Guide Pyramid was replaced by an updated version called MyPyramid in 2005. Both versions of the pyramid featured a triangular diagram divided into sections that showed the recommended daily intake for each major food group.

In June 2011 the USDA replaced the traditional pyramid diagram with a new visual aid called MyPlate. MyPlate looks like a dinner plate divided into sections for four food groups—fruits, vegetables, proteins, and grains—plus a glass depicting dairy. MyPlate shows half of the plate filled with fruits and vegetables, something the USDA emphasizes as a healthy eating habit.

MyPlate is intended to be easier to understand and interpret than the earlier food pyramids. "MyPlate is an uncomplicated symbol to help remind people to think about their food choices in order to lead healthier lifestyles," explained Secretary of Agriculture Tom Vilsack. "This effort is about more than just giving information, it is a matter of making people understand there are options and practical ways to apply them to their daily lives."[47] The MyPlate campaign targets childhood obesity by providing families with an easy way to understand proper daily nutrition. MyPlate can be used in conjunction with the Let's Move initiative to help promote healthy eating habits along with exercise.

Restaurants Heed Calls for Change

Under pressure from the federal government and consumer groups, some fast-food and full-service restaurant chains are also responding to the problem of childhood obesity. In 2011 Darden Restaurants Inc. announced that it planned to provide healthier menu choices at the nineteen hundred restaurants it operates in forty-nine states. Darden's popular restaurant brands include Olive Garden, Red Lobster, LongHorn Steakhouse, Capital Grille, Bahama Breeze, and Seasons 52. Darden pledged to reduce the calories and sodium in all of its meals by 10 percent within five years, and by 20 percent

MyPlate

The U.S. Department of Agriculture's MyPlate diagram shows the amount of each food group Americans are recommended to eat daily.

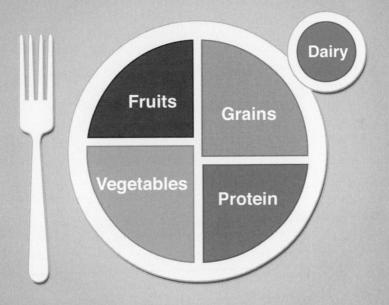

Taken from: United States Dept. of Agriculture. ChooseMyPlate.gov. www.choosemyplate.gov/images/MyPlateImages/PDF/myplate_green.pdf.

within a decade. For its children's meals, Darden planned to stop providing french fries as a side dish and to offer a standard fruit or vegetable side instead. The restaurant chain also planned to serve 1 percent milk with all children's meals unless its young customers ordered an alternative drink.

Several fast-food chains also announced healthy changes to their menus in 2011. McDonald's decided to add a serving of fruit or vegetables to all of its Happy Meals and to reduce the portion size of its french fries. The new children's meals—which may feature apple slices, carrots, raisins, pineapple slices, or mandarin oranges—average 20 percent fewer calories than the previous versions.

In 2011 Darden Restaurants Inc. announced plans to provide healthier menu choices in its nineteen-hundred restaurants, pledging to reduce calories and sodium in all meals by 10 percent within five years.

Another fast-food chain, Arby's, announced that its new Kids Meal will automatically include apple slices with a strawberry yogurt dipping sauce as a side item rather than french fries. Arby's also planned to offer several healthier beverage choices, including low-fat white milk, 100 percent fruit juice, or bottled water. Although french fries and soda will still be available, customers must specifically request them when ordering. The new Kids Meals have an estimated 40 percent fewer calories, 70 percent less total fat, and 50 percent less sodium compared with Arby's previous Kids Meal offerings.

State and Local Initiatives

Some state and city governments have also passed laws and launched campaigns to fight childhood obesity. In 2010, for instance, the state of California passed a law requiring all public school districts to provide students with access to free, fresh drinking water at mealtimes in school food-service areas. The legislation came in response to a survey by the California Department of Public Health's Leaders Encouraging Activity and Nutrition (LEAN) showing that approximately 40 percent of the state's school districts did not provide students with access to free drinking water. In remarks praising the law, then-governor Arnold Schwarzenegger stressed the importance of getting kids to drink water instead of sugar-sweetened beverages as a way to prevent obesity and improve long-term health.

In another example, the city of Tacoma, Washington, partnered with Subway Restaurants to increase the nutritional value of the summer lunches it provides to low-income children under the National School Breakfast and Lunch Programs. Tacoma area children who might otherwise go hungry receive free, well-balanced lunches and snacks at local parks and playgrounds. "While ensuring children have food to eat is a vital first step, what we are feeding them is even more important," said Shon Sylvia, director of recreation and community services for Metro Parks Tacoma. "We made the decision to invest more in the summer food program to express our commitment to the health and well-being of our community."[48]

Many school districts across the United States are also taking steps to fight childhood obesity. The public school system in New Haven, Connecticut, for instance, used a grant from the Whole Kids Foundation to install salad bars in thirty-three school lunchrooms in 2011. The addition of these new salad bars means that 85 percent of the New Haven public schools will have salad bars, which have been proven to increase students' consumption of

FOOD FACT

In 2010 the soft-drink producer Pepsico announced that it would remove its full-calorie drink products from schools in more than two hundred countries by 2012.

Chocolate Milk War

In some school districts, discussions about whether to ban chocolate milk and other sweetened milk from lunchrooms have spiraled into major controversies. The school districts of Fairfax County, Virginia, and Washington, D.C., banned chocolate milk from their elementary schools in 2011 in an effort to promote better student health. This decision, however, prompted a flurry of angry letters and petitions from many students, parents, nutritionists, and influential special-interest groups. Critics argued that even though chocolate milk contains more sugar than regular milk, it is still a healthy option for children because it contains the same vitamins and minerals that fuel bone and muscle growth.

The backlash convinced Fairfax County officials to reverse their decision and reintroduce chocolate milk in school cafeterias. The new chocolate milk is a low-fat version that is sweetened with sucrose, which is made from sugarcane or sugar beets, instead of high-fructose corn syrup. This compromise did not satisfy everyone, however. "If we want to fix childhood obesity, chocolate milk is just one of the things we need to get rid of," said Jeff Anderson, a parent of three students in the district. "It's a treat, not something you have every day with lunch."

Kevin Sieff. "Chocolate Milk Stirs Controversy." *Washington Post*, April 7, 2011. www.washingtonpost.com /local/education/chocolate-milk-stirs-controversy-in -schools/2011/04/07/AF6QB6MD_story.html.

In some U.S. school districts, bans of chocolate milk have stirred controversy. Critics argue that while low-fat chocolate milk contains more sugar than regular milk, it is still a good source of vitamins and minerals.

fresh fruits and vegetables. New Haven had already banned soda from its schools and taken steps to include more whole grains and fewer processed foods in its school lunches. "Kids consume 35 to 50 percent of their daily calories during the school day," explains U.S. representative Rosa DeLauro of

Connecticut. "What you do here addresses the epidemic of obesity and hunger."[49]

Fighting Obesity Around the World

Many countries besides the United States are developing new programs to combat the problem of childhood obesity. England, for example, has childhood obesity rates similar to those of the United States. In response, many local councils across England have implemented policies designed to discourage poor eating habits. An approach taken by some communities involves banning new fast-food restaurants (known as takeaways in England) from opening within 400 yards (385.7m) of any school, park, or youth club. "There's a strong association between fast-food places and young people eating unhealthily when they are ravenous, both at lunchtime and after school,"[50] explains Terry Wheeler, a council member who helped pass the first of these laws in East London.

Canada's program Kids in the Kitchen provides lessons and demonstrations for preparation of healthy foods. The goal is to empower young people to make healthy lifestyle choices.

France is one country that seems to be making headway in the fight against childhood obesity. After decades of increase, the obesity rates among French children ages three to seventeen remained stable between 2000 and 2007, thanks in part to a slate of new laws and programs implemented by the national government. These measures included banning all vending machines from schools, banning misleading television and print advertising for food products, and imposing a 1.5 percent tax on the advertising budgets of food companies that did not encourage healthy eating.

Canada has attacked rising rates of childhood obesity through a program called Kids in the Kitchen, which was introduced in 2006 by the Junior League Association. In partnership with local community organizations, chefs, and nutritionists, Kids in the Kitchen provides lessons and demonstrations related to the preparation of healthy meals and snacks. Its goal is to empower youth to make healthy lifestyle choices in order to reduce childhood obesity rates across the country.

Jamie Oliver's Revolution

One internationally famous chef has made it his personal mission to change the way the world eats. Jamie Oliver, an English chef and star of the television series *The Naked Chef,* tries to convince people to eat healthier and support healthy initiatives in their communities. "Our kids are growing up overweight and malnourished from a diet of processed foods, and today's children will be the first generation ever to live shorter lives than their parents," declared Oliver. "It's time for change. It's time for a Food Revolution. The problem stems from the loss of cooking skills at home and the availability of processed foods at every turn, from the school cafeteria to church function halls, factories, and offices."[51]

Although Oliver promotes healthy eating worldwide, his Food Revolution movement mainly targets the United States, where he now resides with his children. The movement's goals include setting up a nationwide network of community kitchens where anyone can go to learn basic home-cooking skills, persuading schools to provide healthy meals to stu-

The Food Revolution Goes to the United Nations

After launching his Food Revolution in the United States, Chef Jamie Oliver expanded his anti-obesity campaign worldwide. In 2011 he published an open letter to Ban Ki-moon, the secretary general of the United Nations (UN), calling on the UN to join the fight. "I have spent many years now working in schools and communities and talking to governments in the U.S., Britain, and Australia, campaigning against the epidemic of obesity which is threatening the lives of our children," he wrote. "People still don't realize that the problem is not just limited to rich countries, that worldwide being obese or overweight now causes more deaths than under-nutrition." Oliver encouraged the UN to use its resources and influence to help nations around the world halt the epidemic of childhood obesity and ensure a healthy future for the next generation.

Alex Spillius. "Jamie Oliver Takes Children's Diets Bid to UN." *Telegraph* (UK), September 20, 2011. www.telegraph.co.uk/foodanddrink/foodanddrinknews/8777379 /Jamie-Oliver-takes-childrens-diets-bid-to-UN.html.

dents, promoting cooking lessons in schools, convincing restaurants to serve healthier foods, and ensuring that food products are labeled in an honest way.

One of Oliver's major Food Revolution campaigns aims to convince schools to stop serving chocolate milk and other flavored milk. He argues that flavored milk can contain up to twice as much sugar as regular low-fat milk, and that drinking sugary beverages is a habit that increases the risk of obesity. Oliver organized a 2011 protest called the Flavored Milk Day of Action to raise public awareness and gather support for his campaign to end the serving of flavored milk in schools. Several of these local efforts actually produced significant changes in school district policies. In the Palos Verdes Unified School District in Southern California, for instance, a group of parents convinced the

After launching his Food Revolution in the United States, chef Jamie Oliver (pictured) presented it to the United Nations, encouraging the organization to use its resources to fight childhood obesity worldwide.

district's food-services director to eliminate all flavored milk from elementary school meals during a four-month trial period. But many other school districts have resisted the idea. Critics of Oliver's initiative contend that eliminating flavored milk as an option causes students to drink less milk. A dairy-industry study showed that overall milk consumption dropped by 35 percent in elementary schools that eliminated flavored milk. Since flavored milk contains the same essential nutrients as regular milk, critics view such a decline in consumption as a troubling development.

Oliver's foundation also sponsors an educational program called the Big Rig Teaching Kitchen to help people learn to prepare easy, tasty, and healthy meals at home. The Big Rig is a truck equipped with eight cooking stations and six ovens. It travels to different locations and offers classes for adults, kindergarten through twelfth grade students, and families. Oliver hopes his truck and other programs spur families in the United States and throughout the world to change their eating patterns and exercise habits and thus reduce the rate of childhood obesity.

Introduction: A Modern Childhood

1. David Katz. "Irresponsible, Lazy, Stupid Gluttony! (or . . . Larger Forces)." *Huffington Post,* September 16, 2011. www.huffingtonpost.com /david-katz-md/the-economy-and -obesity_b_963823.html.

2. Claudia Kalb. "Culture of Corpulence." *Newsweek,* March 13, 2010. www.thedailybeast.com/news week/2010/03/13/culture-of-corpu lence.html

3. Lesley Kinzel. "Fat Kids, Cruel World." *Newsweek,* April 19, 2010. www.thedailybeast.com/news week/2010/04/19/fat-kids-cruel -world.html.

Chapter 1: A Growing Problem

4. Quoted in Madison Park. "How Does a Baby Get Fat?" CNN, June 27, 2011. www.cnn.com/2011/HEALTH /06/27/obese.toddlers/index.html.

5. Amber J. Hammons and Barbara H. Fiese. "Is Frequency of Shared Family Meals Related to the Nutritional Health of Children and Adolescents?" *Pediatrics*, May 2, 2011.

http://pediatrics.aappublications .org/content/127/6/e1565.full.

6. Ben Dyson and Lisa Dyson. "Recess Should Not Be Optional Program." *Commercial Appeal*, January 21, 2009. www.commercialappeal.com /news/2009/jan/21/recess-should -not-be-optional/.

7. Quoted in Rick Nauert. "Stress Contributes to Childhood Obesity." *PsychCentral,* May 15, 2009. http://psychcentral.com/news /2009/05/15/stress-contributes-to -childhood-obesity/5926.html.

8. Quoted in *ScienceDaily.* "Obesity Associated with Depression and Vice Versa." March 2, 2011. www.sciencedaily.com/releases /2010/03/100301165728.htm.

9. Quoted in Jan Jarvis. "Obesity Among Poor Children Tied to Diet." *Times Leader,* November 19, 2008. www.timesleader.com/news /Obesity_among_poor_children _tied_to_diet_11-19-2008.html.

10. Quoted in Park. "How Does a Baby Get Fat?"

11. Quoted in Park. "How Does a Baby Get Fat?"

12. Quoted in *New York Times Upfront.* "What We Eat," May 4, 2009. http:// teacher.scholastic.com/scholastic

news/indepth/upfront/features /index.asp?article=f050409_Eat.

13. Quoted in *New York Times Upfront,* "What We Eat."

Chapter 2: Are You Obese?

14. Quoted in Robert Pretlow. *Overweight: What Kids Say.* Charleston, NC: CreateSpace, 2010, p. 161.

15. Quoted in *ScienceDaily.* "Pediatricans Can Help Parents Recognize Overweight Preschoolers," June 15, 2010. www.sciencedaily.com/ releases/2010/06/100615141747 .htm.

16. Quoted in Alexa Pozniak. "Schools Test Children's Body Fat." ABC News. www.abcnews.go.com/Health /story?id=117278&page=1.

17. Quoted in ABC News. "The Life of an Obese Teenager." www.abc news.go.com/Primetime/story ?id=132027&page=1.

18. Quoted in Karen Springen. "Fatgirl Slim." *Newsweek,* May 18, 2008. www.thedailybeast.com/news week/2008/05/18/fatgirl slim.html.

19. Quoted in Sandra G. Boodman. "Parenting an Overweight Child Can Be Difficult." *Washington Post,* March 21, 2011. www.washington post.com/wp-dyn/content/article /2011/03/21/AR2011032103815 .html.

20. Quoted in Springen. "Fatgirl Slim."

21. Quoted in Jeff Barnes. "Weight Loss for Kids." Stop Obesity Now, December 31, 2010. www.stop-childhood -obesity.com/weight-loss.html.

22. Quoted in Healthy Journey. "Getting Help for Obese Children." www.healthy-journey.com/getting -help-for-obese-children.

23. Quoted in Nojan Aminosharei. "Into the Fire." *Elle,* August 3, 2010. www.elle.com/Pop-Culture /Celebrity-Spotlight/Demi-Lovato -Interview.

24. Quoted in Pretlow, p. 56.

25. Quoted in Pretlow, p. 86.

26. Quoted in Pretlow, p. 90.

Chapter 3: Endangering Lives

27. Quoted in Rebecca Smith. "Obese Children Suffering High Blood Pressure." *Telegraph* (UK), August 22, 2007. www.telegraph.co.uk/news /uknews/1560994/Obese-children -suffering-high-blood-pressure .html.

28. Quoted in Sally Chew. "Study: Obese Children, Teens Have the Arteries of 45-Year-Olds." CNN, November 12, 2008. articles.cnn .com/2008-11-12/health/obese.teen .arteries_1_geetha-raghuveer-child hood-obesity-obese-children?_s =PM:HEALTH.

29. Quoted in American Heart Association. "Overweight in Children," March 29, 2011. www.heart .org/HEARTORG/GettingHealthy /Overweight-in-Children_UCM _304054_Article.jsp.

30. Quoted in Jeanna Bryner. "Heavy Kids, Heavy Emotions." MSNBC, February 14, 2010. www.msnbc

.msn.com/id/35369009/ns/health-kids_and_parenting/t/heavy-kids-heavy-emotions.

31. Quoted in Alanah Eriksen. "I'm Anorexic Again. . . . I Have a Phobia of Eating More than 400 Calories: Nikki Grahame on Her Eating Disorder." *Daily Mail* (UK), October 26, 2011. www.dailymail.co.uk/tvshowbiz/article-2053286/Nikki-Grahame-anorexia-I-phobia-eating-400-calories.html#ixzz1bzVauXdN.

32. Quoted in Jeanna Bryner. "Childhood Obesity Takes Psychological Toll, Too." *Live Science,* February 14, 2010. www.livescience.com/6126-childhood-obesity-takes-psychological-toll.html.

33. Quoted in ABC News. "The Life of an Obese Teenager." www.abcnews.go.com/Primetime/story?id=132027&page=1.

Chapter 4: Reclaiming Health

34. Deepak Chopra. "Ending Diets That Don't Actually Work: How People Actually Lost Weight." *Huffington Post,* September 21, 2011. www.huffingtonpost.com/deepak-chopra/obesity-habits_b_966873.html.

35. Quoted in More4Kids. "A Family Solution to Childhood Obesity," 2009. health.more4kids.info/2009/01/a-family-solution-to-childhood-obesity.

36. Annemarie Colbin. "Fat-Free Food: A Bad Idea." *Food and Healing,*

1997. www.foodandhealing.com/articles/article-fatfreebad.htm.

37. Kristi Kingston. "Changing Eating Habits for a Healthier Family." *Austin Statesman,* March 12, 2011. www.statesman.com/life/changing-eating-habits-for-a-healthier-family-1315209.html.

38. Kingston, "Changing Eating Habits for a Healthier Family."

39. Livestrong. "Five Things You Need to Know About Weight Loss Programs for Teens," August 11, 2011. www.livestrong.com/article/5268-need-weight-loss-programs-teens/#ixzz1Z59HF4ft.

40. Quoted in Wellspring Camps. "Fat Camps: Why Wellspring Is a Better Choice for Your Child." www.wellspringcamps.com/why.html.

41. Quoted in Camp Shane Diet Resorts. "Camp Shane Weight Loss Success Story," 2009. www.campshane.com/blog/index.php/camp-shane-weight-loss-camp-success-story.

42. Quoted in Jessica Fryman. "Gym for Kids and Family Helps Las Vegas Residents Stay Trim." *Las Vegas Review Journal,* September 27, 2011. www.lvrj.com/view/gym-for-kids-family-helps-las-vegas-residents-stay-trim-together-130615043.html?ref=043.

43. Quoted in Fryman, "Gym for Kids and Family."

44. Quoted in Anne Harding. "Surgery Is No Quick Fix for Obese Teens." CNN, June 22, 2011. www.cnn.com/2011/HEALTH/06/22/surgery.obese.teens/index.html.

Chapter 5: A Revolution Against Obesity

45. Quoted in Lee Ferran. "Michelle Obama: 'Let's Move' Initiative Battles Childhood Obesity." ABC News, February 9, 2010. abcnews.go.com/GMA/Health/michelle-obama-childhood-obesity-initiative/story?id=9781473.

46. Quoted in The White House. "President Obama Signs Healthy Hunger-Free Kids Act of 2010 into Law," December 13, 2010. www.whitehouse.gov/the-press-office/2010/12/13/president-obama-signs-healthy-hunger-free-kids-act-2010-law.

47. Quoted in USDA. "First Lady, Agriculture Secretary Launch *MyPlate* Icon as a New Reminder to Help Consumers to Make Healthier Food Choices," June 2, 2011. www.cnpp.usda.gov/Publications/MyPlate/PressRelease.pdf.

48. Quoted in PR Newswire. "Metro Parks Tacoma and Subway Restaurants Join Forces in the Fight against Childhood Obesity," July 1, 2011. www.prnewswire.com/news-releases/metro-parks-tacoma-and-subway-restaurants-partner-in-the-fight-against-childhood-obesity-124640498.

49. Quoted in Allan Appel. "Count 'Em: 33 School Salad Bars Debut." *New Haven Independent*, September 28, 2011. www.newhavenindependent.org/index.php/archives/entry/vegetables.

50. Quoted in Denis Campbell. "Takeaway Ban Near Schools to Help Fight Child Obesity." *Observer* (UK), February 27, 2010. www.guardian.co.uk/society/2010/feb/28/takeaway-food-school-ban.

51. Jamie Oliver. "Jamie Oliver's Food Revolution." Jamie Oliver Foundation. www.jamieoliver.com/us/foundation/jamies-food-revolution/about.

bariatric surgery: A medical procedure performed on the stomach and/or intestines to help a person with extreme obesity lose weight.

body mass index (BMI): A numerical figure calculated using a person's height and weight that provides an indication of body fat percentage and health risk.

bulimia: A condition in which bouts of overeating are followed by purging the body of the excess calories consumed, usually through self-induced vomiting, use of laxatives, or extreme exercise.

calorie: A unit of energy-producing potential in food; if not burned by the body's metabolic processes, this energy is converted to fat and stored in the body.

cholesterol: A steroid produced in the liver or intestines that aids in cell function; a diet high in saturated fats can lead to high cholesterol levels in the bloodstream, which increases the risk of heart disease.

diabetes: A medical disorder in which the body loses the ability to produce or use the hormone insulin, which is necessary for converting sugar into energy.

metabolism: The series of processes by which the body converts food into energy and waste products.

obese: Having a body weight more than 20 percent higher than recommended for a person's height and build, or having a body mass index greater than thirty; being obese increases a person's risk of several serious illnesses, including diabetes and heart disease.

overweight: Having a higher body weight than is considered healthy for a person's height and build, or having a body mass index greater than twenty-five but less than thirty.

sedentary: An inactive lifestyle that is characterized by little to no exercise and a great deal of sitting.

self-esteem: A person's confidence in his or her own value as an individual.

sucrose: The organic compound commonly known as sugar.

ORGANIZATIONS TO CONTACT

American Academy of Pediatrics (AAP)

141 Northwest Point Blvd.
Elk Grove Village, IL 60007-1098
phone: (847) 434-4000
website: www.aap.org

The AAP is an organization of sixty thousand pediatricians committed to the attainment of optimal physical, mental, and social health and well-being for all infants, children, adolescents, and young adults. The AAP website provides information on how the organization is fighting childhood obesity.

Centers for Disease Control and Prevention (CDC)

1600 Clifton Rd.
Atlanta, GA 30333
phone: (800) 232-4636
website: www.cdc.gov

This U.S. government agency is dedicated to protecting Americans' health and promoting their quality of life through the prevention and control of disease, injury, and disability. The CDC maintains a website that provides the latest statistics and information about childhood obesity, its causes, consequences, and cures.

Obesity Society

8757 Georgia Ave., Ste. 1320
Silver Spring, MD 20910
phone: (301) 563-6526
website: www.obesity.org

The Obesity Society is a leading scientific organization dedicated to the study of obesity. Since its founding in 1982, the society has encouraged research on the causes and treatment of obesity and kept the medical community and the public informed of new advances.

Robert Wood Johnson Foundation
Center to Prevent Childhood Obesity

Route 1 and College Rd. E.
PO Box 2316
Princeton, NJ 08543
phone: (877) 843-7953
website: www.reversechildhoodobesity.org

This national organization is dedicated to reversing the childhood obesity epidemic by changing public food policies and creating healthier environments in schools and communities.

Shape Up America!

PO Box 149
Clyde Park, MT 59018
phone: (406) 686-4844
website: www.shapeup.org

Shape Up America! is a nonprofit organization committed to raising awareness of obesity as a health issue and to providing information on healthy weight management. Its website features information and ideas to help people achieve a healthy weight.

World Health Organization (WHO)

Avenue Appia 20
1211 Geneva 27
Switzerland
phone: 41 22 791 21 11
website: www.who.int

WHO is the authority for health within the United Nations. It is responsible for providing leadership on international health matters, including childhood obesity.

Books

Abby Ellin. *Teenage Waistland: A Former Fat Kid Weighs In on Living Large, Losing Weight, and How Parents Can (and Can't) Help.* Jackson, TN: Public Affairs, 2005. Ellin's autobiography describes what it was like growing up overweight and offers advice for parents seeking to help their overweight children.

Anne M. Fletcher. *Weight Loss Confidential: How Teens Lose Weight and Keep It Off—And What They Wish Parents Knew.* Boston: Houghton Mifflin Harcourt, 2008. Written by a doctor, this book offers tips for teens who are trying to lose weight from teens who have succeeded in doing so.

Susan Okie. *Fed Up! Winning the War against Childhood Obesity.* Washington, DC: Joseph Henry, 2006. This book examines the causes and consequences of childhood obesity in medical terms as well as through personal anecdotes.

Miriam B. Vos. *The No-Diet Obesity Solution for Kids.* Bethesda, MD: AGA Institute, 2009. Written by a doctor, this book provides practical and positive advice for families with overweight children, along with more than sixty kid-friendly healthy recipes.

Websites

Let's Move (www.letsmove.gov). This website provides details on First Lady Michelle Obama's initiative to fight childhood obesity. It describes programs available nationwide to improve American children's fitness and nutrition.

President's Council on Fitness and Nutrition (www.fitness.gov). This website provides information on the U.S. government's programs to promote fitness among children in American schools.

Weigh2Rock (www.weigh2rock.com). A good source of online health and weight-loss education. It also features an online support community of several thousand overweight children, teenagers, and parents from around the world.

INDEX

A

AAP. *See* American Academy of Pediatrics

Acanthosis nigricans, 32

Adolescents. *See* Children/adolescents

American Academy of Child and
    Adolescent Psychiatry, 20

American Academy of Pediatrics (AAP),
    18, 30, 33–34, 37

American Heart Association, 48

Anorexia, 55–56

Applied Developmental Science (journal),
    52–53

Arby's restaurants, 82

B

Bariatric surgery, 70

The Biggest Loser (TV program), 66

BMI. *See* Body mass index

Body fat
    body mass index and, 30
    measuring for, *36*
    use in determining physical education
        grades, 36–37

Body mass index (BMI), 30–32
    as indicator for weight-loss surgery,
        72
    measuring for, *36*
    percentiles, by age, *31*

Breastfeeding, benefits of, 17

Bulimia, 54–55

Bullying, 10, 42–43, 56–57

C

California Department of Public Health,
    83

Canada, prevention program in, 86

Cardiovascular disease, 48–49

Centers for Disease Control and
    Prevention (CDC), 30
    anti-childhood obesity program of, 79
    on breastfeeding, 17
    on medical costs related to obesity, 59
    on prevalence of obesity among
        children/adolescents, 32
    on probability of adult obesity for
        obese children, 50

CHAMP (Child Health Assessment and
    Monitoring Program, NC), 35

Chefs Move to School program, 77

Child Health Assessment and Monitoring
    Program (CHAMP, NC), 35

Childhood Obesity Demonstration Project
    (Centers for Disease Control and
    Prevention), 79

Children/adolescents, obesity among
    prevalence of, 9, 12, *22*, 32
    trends in, *15*

Children's Defense Fund, 14, 21, 53

China, prevalence of child obesity/
    overweight in, 27

Cholesterol, 48–49

Chopra, Deepak, 61

Commercial Appeal (newspaper), 17

Cutting Myself in Half (LeBaron), 51

D

Darden Restaurants Inc., 80–81
Department of Agriculture, U.S. (USDA), 80, 81
Department of Health and Human Services, U.S., 32
Depression, 18–19, 57
Diabetes (journal), 24
Diabetes, type 2, 48
Diet Tribe (TV program), 66
Diet(s)
    American, changes in, 8–9
    extreme, 53
    of low-income youth, 22–23
    making changes in, 63, 65
    Mediterranean, 28
    obesity crisis worsened by changes in, 13–16
Drugs, weight-loss, 73

E

Eating disorders, 41–42, 54–56
Economic(s)
    costs of obesity, *59*, 59–60
    as factor in overweight/obesity, 22–23
Emotional problems, 41–43, 51–53
England, prevention programs in, 85
Entertainment media, time spent by adolescents using, 23
Exercise, 68–70
    addiction to, 56
    among youth, 12
    lack of, 16–18
Extreme Makeover (TV program), 66

F

Fast foods/fast-food restaurants
    consumption of, 8, 13–14, 23
    inclusion of toys with, 25

    response to childhood obesity problem by, 80–82
    restrictions on, 85
Flavored Milk Day of Action, 87–88
Food and Drug Administration, U.S. (FDA), 73
Food, Family, and Farming Foundation, 77
Food Guide Pyramid, 80
Food Revolution movement, 86–89
France, prevention programs in, 86
Frist, Bill, 78–79
Fruit and Vegetable Alliance, 77

G

Gastric banding, 70
Gastric bypass procedure, 71–72
Grahame, Nikki, 55
Greece, 28
Greek Childhood Obesity (GRECO) study, 28

H

Health impacts, 9–10, 24, 46–50, 60
Healthy, Hunger-Free Kids Act (2010), 78–79
Healthy Journey (website), 41
Hypertension (high blood pressure), 46–47

I

I Used to Be Fat (TV program), 66
The Importance of Family Dinners VI (National Center on Addiction and Substance Abuse), 16
Infants/toddlers
    benefits of breastfeeding for, 17
    prevalence of overweight among, 24
Institute of Medicine, U.S., 24
Insulin, 48

T

Task Force on Childhood Obesity, 77
Taveras, Elsie, 12, 24
Television
    limiting, 63
    time spent watching, 18, 23
    weight loss as topic on, 66
Trevino, Roberto, 22, 23

U

United Fresh Produce Association,
    77
United Nations, 87
United States
    economy, impact of obesity on,
        75–76
    percentage of health costs related to
        obesity in, 59
    prevalence of obesity in, 9
University of Michigan, 48
University of North Carolina, 13
University of South Florida, 34
USDA (U.S. Department of Agriculture),
    80, 81

V

Vilsack, Tom, 80

W

Weight loss
    diet pills and, 73
    extreme methods of, 54
    as means of taking control, 58
    online resources for, 43–45
    as topic for TV shows, 66
Weight-loss camps, 65, 67–68
Weight-loss surgery, 44, 70–72
Weight2Rock (website), 43
Wellspring camps, 67
Whole Kids Foundation, 83
World Health Organization (WHO), 9,
    12

Y

YMCAs, 68

Z

Zampelas, Antonis, 28

PICTURE CREDITS

Cover: © Gerald Bernard/Shutterstock
.com; © iingles/Shutterstock.com;
© Joao Virissimo/Shutterstock.com

© amphotos/Alamy, 34

© Angela Hampton Picture Library/
Alamy, 64

AP Images/Larry Crowe, 85

AP Images/Nam Y. Huh, 84

AP Images/PRNewsFoto/Darden
Restaurants, Inc., 82

© Art Directors & TRIP/Alamy, 25

© Aurora Photos/Alamy, 13

© Benedicte Desrus/Alamy, 49, 71

© Bubbles Photography/Alamy, 14, 56

© Catchlight Visual Services/Alamy, 19,
58

© Chad Ehlers/Alamy, 62

Cristina Pedrazzini/Photo
Researchers, Inc., 55

© D. Hurst/Alamy, 73

Gale/Cengage Learning, 15, 22, 31, 33,
59, 81

Gusto/Photo Researchers, Inc., 47

Holly Farrell/ABC-TV/The Kobal
Collection/Art Resource, NY, 88

© Janet Jensen/Tacoma News Tribune/
MCT via Getty Images, 69

© Kevin Winter/Getty Images, 42

© Leila Cutler/Alamy, 39

© Nikki Kahn/The Washington Post
via Getty Images, 79

© Oote Boe Photography 1/Alamy,
27

© Paul J. Richards/AFP/Getty Images,
66

© Peter Dazeldy/Photographer's
Choice/Getty Images, 36

Phanie/Photo Researchers, Inc., 30

© Saul Loeb/AFP/Getty Images, 78

© Stockfolio®/Alamy, 21

© Stuwdamdorp/Alamy, 76

© Thomas Imo/Alamy, 52

Tony Craddock/Photo Researchers,
Inc., 10

ABOUT THE AUTHOR

Leanne Currie-McGhee is married to Keith McGhee and is the proud mother of Hope and Grace. She and her family live in Norfolk, Virginia, where she has written children's books for ten years.